THE

ROMAN CATHOLIC
CHURCH'S ARROGANT
FALSE CLAIMS

THE
ROMAN CATHOLIC
CHURCH'S ARROGANT
FALSE CLAIMS

HENDRICK PARK

THE ROMAN CATHOLIC CHURCH'S ARROGANT FALSE CLAIMS

The Holy Bible, English Standard Version Copyright © 2001 by Crossway Bibles, a publishing ministry of Good News Publishers.

Holy Bible, New International Version®, NIV® Copyright ©1973, 1978, 1984, 2011 by Biblica, Inc.® Used by permission. All rights reserved worldwide.

iUniverse books may be ordered through booksellers or by contacting:

iUniverse
1663 Liberty Drive
Bloomington, IN 47403
www.iuniverse.com
1-800-Authors (1-800-288-4677)

Because of the dynamic nature of the Internet, any web addresses or links contained in this book may have changed since publication and may no longer be valid. The views expressed in this work are solely those of the author and do not necessarily reflect the views of the publisher, and the publisher hereby disclaims any responsibility for them.

Any people depicted in stock imagery provided by Thinkstock are models, and such images are being used for illustrative purposes only. Certain stock imagery © Thinkstock.

ISBN: 978-1-5320-1110-8 (sc)
ISBN: 978-1-5320-1109-2 (e)

Library of Congress Control Number: 2016919388

Print information available on the last page.

iUniverse rev. date: 11/23/2016

CONTENTS

PREFACE

THE ROMAN CATHOLIC CHURCH IS the largest Christian Church. Roughly one half of the Christians in the world are the Catholics. Regrettably, however, this Catholic Church is not true and faithful to the Bible (the Holy Scripture). There are not a few things in the Catholic Church which we do not read in the Bible. We read in Isaiah 34:16,

Seek and Read from the Book of the Lord:

Not one of these shall be missing;
None shall be without her mate.

For the mouth of the Lord has commanded, and His Spirit has gathered them.

Some of the doctrines and the structure and the claims of the Catholic Church are not found in the Bible.

Our Lord Jesus Christ admitted the authority of the Bible. (Matthew 4:4, 7, 10). Therefore, the Christians should live according to the Bible and the Christian Church should be managed according to the Bible. Sadly, however, there are many things in the Catholic Church which are contradictory to the Biblical teaching. The author of this book tried to enumerate them in this book.

I

THE CATHOLIC CHURCH'S ARROGANT FALSE CLAIMS

A YOUNG MAN WHO LIVES IN a small town in Ontario, Canada liked a pretty girl who lived nearby and said to her: "The Holy Spirit told me to marry Kathy." Kathy is the name of the girl. But Kathy did not hear anything from the Holy Spirit of God. So she did not believe what the young man said to her and refused to marry him.

This narrative is not a fiction this writer made up, but is a real story. The real name of the girl was not Kathy. Kathy did not believe what the young man said to her. She knew that the young man was telling a lie. So she said to him: The Holy Spirit told me, "Do not marry him."

The reason I tell this narrative is not to tell an interesting story. I have an important purpose. My purpose is to let the readers know that the Catholic Church makes arrogant claims and that they are false claims. The false claims of the Roman Catholic Church, in my personal view, resemble, in some respects, what the young man said to the girl. The young man said to the girl, "The Holy Spirit told me to marry Kathy." My purpose is also to let the readers know that the Catholic Church makes numerous arrogant false claims and that they have no Biblical ground. To express simply, my purpose is to let the readers know what True Christianity is. If the readers read the Bible (the Holy Scripture) carefully, you will know whether the claims of the Catholic Church are true or false. In Christianity that has come from God, only the Bible is the standard and true criterion. Jesus Christ our Lord recognized the authority of the Bible. (Matthew 4:1-11) The Bible was provided by God.

> "Seek and read from the book of the Lord: Not one of these shall be missing; none shall be without her mate. For the mouth of the Lord has commanded, and His Spirit has gathered them." (Isaiah 34:16)

Here I would like to introduce for the readers a few of the arrogant false claims of the Roman Catholic Church. These claims are included in CATECHISM OF THE CATHOLIC CHURCH which was officially published by the Catholic Church.

No.846 in the Catechism says, "Outside the Church there is no salvation." (The Church here refers to the Catholic Church.)

The Catechism continues, "How are we to understand this affirmation? Re-formulated positively, it means that all salvation comes from Christ the Head through the Church which is His Body ... The Church, a pilgrim now on earth, is necessary for salvation. Christ is present to us in His Body which is the Church ... Hence they would not be saved who, knowing that the Catholic Church was founded as necessary by God through Christ, would refuse either to enter or to remain in it."

No.830 in the Catechism says, "Where there is Christ Jesus, there is the Catholic Church." In her subsists the fullness of Christ's body united with its head; this implies that she receives from him "the fullness of the means of salvation" which he has willed: correct and complete confession of faith, full sacramental life and ordained ministry in apostolic succession.

No.981 in the Catechism says, "The Church has received the keys of the Kingdom of heaven so that, in her, sins may be forgiven through Christ's blood and the Holy Spirit action." (The Church here refers to the Catholic Church.)

No.982 in the Catechism says, "There is no offense, however serious, that the Church cannot forgive." (The Church here refers to the Catholic Church.)

No.882 in the Catechism says, The Pope, Bishop of Rome and Peter's successor, "is the perpetual and visible source and foundation of the unity both of bishops and of the whole company of the faithful." "For the Roman Pontiff, by reason of his office as Vicar of Christ, and as pastor of the entire Church has full, supreme, and universal power over the whole Church, a power which he can always exercise unhindered."

No.883 in the Catechism says, "The college or body of bishops has no authority unless united with the Roman Pontiff, Peter's successor, as its head." As such this college has "supreme and full authority over the universal Church; but this power cannot be exercised without the agreement of the Roman Pontiff."

No.119 in the Catechism says, "It is the task of exegete to work, according to these rules, toward a better understanding and explanation of the meaning of Sacred Scripture in order that their research may help the Church to form a firmer judgment. For, of course, all that has been said about the manner of interpreting Scripture is ultimately subject to the judgment of the Church which exercises the divinely conferred commission and ministry of watching over and interpreting the Word of God." (The Church here refers to the Catholic Church.)

No.772 in the Catechism says, "It is in the Church that Christ fulfills and reveals his own mystery as the purpose of God's plan: to unite all things in him." (The Church here refers to the Catholic Church.)

No.776 in the Catechism says, "As sacrament, the Church is Christ's instrument. She is taken up by him also as the instrument for the salvation of all, the universal sacrament of salvation by which

Christ is at once manifesting and actualizing the mystery of God's love for men." (The Church here refers to the Catholic Church.)

No.778 in the Catechism says, "The Church is both the means and the goal of God's plan: prefigured in creation, prepared for in the Old Covenant, founded by the words and actions of Jesus Christ, fulfilled by his redeeming cross and his Resurrection, the Church has been manifested as the mystery of Salvation by the outpouring of the Holy spirit. She will be perfected in the glory of heaven as the assembly of all the redeemed of the earth." (The Church here refers to the Catholic Church.)

No.779 in the Catechism says, "The Church is both visible and spiritual, a hierarchical society and the Mystical Body of Christ. She is one, yet formed of two components, human and divine. That is her mystery, which only faith can accept."

No.780 in the Catechism says, "The Church in this world is the sacrament of salvation, the sign and the instrument of the communion of God and men." (The Church refers to the Catholic Church.)

II

A CRITICAL COMMENT ON THE CATHOLIC CHURCH'S ARROGANT FALSE CLAIMS

THE CATHOLIC CHURCH IS LEGALISTIC and authoritarian in nature and essence. This is antithetic to the Gospel of the New Testament which is personalistic in nature and essence. Christianity is a religion of the grace of God Who is a God of love. We read in Exodus 34:6,

And the Lord descended in the cloud and stood with him (Moses) there and proclaimed the name of the Lord. The Lord passed before him, and proclaimed, "The Lord, the Lord a God merciful and gracious, slow to anger and abounding in steadfast love and faithfulness, keeping steadfast love for thousands, forgiving iniquity and transgression and sin.

So God is a personal God of love.

The evidence that God is a "personal" God is numerous.

For instance,

1. Exodus 34:6
2. Isaiah 54:4-8
3. God is a friend of Abraham. (Isaiah 41:8)
4. God wails, cries and weeps. (Jeremiah 48:31-32)
5. Jesus Christ Who is the Son of God

The ultimate value and reality are to be found in persons, human or Divine. God created man in the image and after the likeness of God Himself. In Genesis 1:26-27 in the Old Testament we read, and then God said, "Let us make man in our image, after our likeness ..." So God created man in His own image. The image in which man was created includes reason, morality, emotion and personality.

Here is a testimony of the Cardinal Eugene Tisserant who is an insider of the Papal Court. He said "I fear that history will reproach the Holy See for having practiced a policy of selfish convenience and little else." Here is another testimony made by the Archbishop Luigi Puecher-Passavalli of Italy. "The experience of members of the Papal Court which I have gained during many years has given me the unshakable convictions that never, never, unto the world's end, are they prepared to renounce worldly power. They will employ every possible means, now public, now secret, now more now less forcible, to put themselves in possession of this power, and that at any price. Not Religion, not Piety, not Christianity, not Theology is the proper interest of the members of the Papal Curia, but the political advantage of a political institution"

Since these are the testimonies of the insiders of the Papal count of the Catholic Church, they are credible and valuable testimonies. The implication of the testimonies is immense. It is, in this writer's view, one of the windows through which you and I can see the inside of the Roman Catholic Church. There are other windows as well. I would like to urge our Catholic friends: "Wake up!!!"

III

THE ROMAN CATHOLIC CHURCH IN HISTORY

THE ROMAN CATHOLIC CHURCH, WITH its 1.1 billion adherents and long history, is the largest and probably most powerful church in the world. The Roman Church is distinct from other Christian denominations, especially from the Protestant churches, in the form of the ecclesiastical government, in worship, in doctrines and theology, and in what we call the character of its religiosity. The papacy is unique with the Roman Church.

The pope Benedict XVI, on July 10, 2007, by approving the document released by the Congregation for the Doctrine of the Faith at the Vatican, reasserted that only the Roman Catholic Church is the true church founded by Christ. The document is, in essence, a restatement of the traditional exclusive absolutist doctrinal position of the Catholic Church. The pope asserted that the Orthodox churches are churches with "defect" because they do not recognize the primacy of the pope; and that other Christian denominations including the Protestant churches are not churches in the proper sense but merely ecclesial communities and therefore did not have the "means of salvation". Benedict's claims created repercussions among the non-Catholic churches in the world.

The present narrative represents a critical appraisal of the papacy and the Roman Catholic Church. It contains historical, biblical and theological investigations. I call the Roman Catholic Church 'the papal church' because the Church has been under the autocratic rule of the pope since the Middle Ages; because the ecclesiastical structure of the Church developed to a large extent according to the will of the pope who desired to establish a church under the papal dominion; and because the pope has exerted influence in the formation of the doctrines of the Catholic Church by way of a legal conception of the Christian religion and through the ecclesiastical, sacramentalist interpretation of the religion, which have contributed to advance the papal power and the power of the priestly caste of which the pope is the head.

This proposition may sound to some readers like an outrageous and unfounded slander. The present volume is a serious attempt to substantiate the above proposition. "Serious" means serious. In the humble opinion of the writer there are sufficient historical and biblical resources to support the proposition.

A critical appraisal of the Catholic Church was not undertaken without much scruple and hard thinking for some time. Using the Holy Scripture and history as the criteria, I considered and reconsidered, and checked the main points again and again. The writer used the Scripture as the principal criterion because the Scripture is accepted by Christianity as the word of God, and as such is regarded as the standard of faith and morals by all major Christian denominations including the Roman Catholic Church.

Also, of course, I have consulted the works of many authorities in the field. I acknowledge that I am deeply indebted to their works in all topics discussed in this book. When I became finally convinced, on the ground of indisputable evidence, of the depth of moral corruption and worldly ambition in the history of the popes, and also when I learned that the papal claims to extraordinary powers do not have a sound biblical and historical basis, nor do several major doctrines which are unique with the Roman Church, and that the papacy itself is a man-made institution established by means of deceit and maneuvers in addition to the historical and geographical conditions which were advantageous for the ambitious bishop of Rome to advance his power, only then had I the courage to write this book and have it published in order to bring all these points out into the open. Untruth and deceit need to be exposed and truth must be upheld. The writer feels it his moral and religious duty to indict the papacy, to expose its deceitfulness and false teachings, and to show how the papacy negatively affected the Roman Catholic Church, transforming it into a religion profoundly different from the Christianity of the New Testament. It is hard to believe that the papacy which needed so much deceit and manipulation to establish and maintain itself is a divine institution founded by Christ. Garry Wills, a Catholic historian, calls the papacy "Structures *of Deceit*" in his book titled Papal Sin (2000). "Structures *of Deceit*" is the subtitle of the book.

It does not take exceptional insight or intelligence to see the duplicity of the popes in past history, especially in the Middle Ages and its harmful impact on the church and the world. It just takes the time to read the history. You will be astounded at the sheer quantity and depth of moral corruption and will wonder how a religious institution can go down to such a low state. It is shocking that such a scandalous thing could take place at all in the history of the Christian Church.

I am mystified by the fact that the papacy and the Roman Catholic Church are still powerful and flourishing despite the extent of deceit and corruption in their history. It is an open question to ask how this has been possible. A vast majority of Catholics do not know and it appears that they do not care to know important historical facts about the papacy and the official Roman Catholic Church.

In the Roman Church the doctrines about the papacy are not isolated, peripheral doctrines, but are integrally linked to major doctrines of the Roman Church. They are part of its articles of faith.

The historical fact of the use of "forgeries" and other forms of deceit has been confirmed by church historians and is verifiable by the careful reader, so it is in a position to discredit and undermine the Catholic Church itself. In this world, even the established institutional religions do not always, so it appears, operate strictly according to the principle of truth. Can the question of truth and untruth be ignored or dealt with casually? Because of the very nature of religion, we cannot avoid facing the question of truth and falsehood; each believer has to make his or her decision about it.

Most Catholic theologians, historians and members of the Church's magisterium (the teaching authority of the Roman Catholic Church) would not be unaware of the historical fact of "forgeries". As in natural science, so in religion, the question of truth is a critical matter and cannot and should not be avoided or covered up. Charles Davis, the leading Catholic theologian in Great Britain, faced the question of truth and could not remain in the Roman Church, and left it in 1966. Davis did not leave the Catholic Church quietly, but made it public. Also the following year he published a book and gave a full account of the reason of his public break with the Catholic Church. The title of the book is *A Question of Conscience*. May we courteously and hesitantly ask the Vatican to provide a public explanation about the use of "the multiple forgeries" and other forms of deceit which are documented in this and other available books?

Moral corruptions in past history, false claims and pretensions would not be unique to the Roman Church. Major institutional religions (e.g. Buddhism and Hinduism) continue to be prosperous and popular. In our humble view, this popularity is mainly due to the ineradicable religiosity and credulity in the human nature.

This credulity has been demonstrated in the history of religions and politics. The credulity, social pressure, conformity, habit or traditionalism are such that once a certain religion is established somehow, it will continue to prosper. Most humans who seek religious comfort do so partly because the reality of life is harsh, and partly because there is a fear of death and what may come after death. Given the religiosity and the gullibility of the masses, and if given enough time, an ambitious strong man or a charismatic leader will be able to tame people and mold their beliefs and outlook in a desired direction by such means as manipulation, the promise of happiness in the next world, indoctrination, impression of authority, political or even military power, ritual and music. Music is a very effective means of exerting influence on people's emotions and minds. A solemn religious rite conducted by clergymen in ornate vestments, accompanied by inspiring music, has much appeal to the aesthetic senses of those present and moves them emotionally. In a closed confessional or ideological environment, the strong man's effort will be even more successful. This is true, to some extent, of the secular state and its dictator or ruling group as well. Nazi Germany, Fascist Italy, Franco's Spain, imperial Japan and the communist states are examples in the 20th century. Examples such as these show that the minds of the masses can be bent. Such efforts can be more successful in religion and the result will last longer because here the efforts are made in the name of a Deity. It is regrettable that in religion the use of the name of a Deity is at the disposal of the clergy for their personal ambition.

The sacred Name of God is profaned by a clergyman when he uses the Name for his personal ambition. He can take advantage of the mysterious power religion has over the minds of people. Religion is a strange thing. The clergy are particularly in danger of that by reason of their responsibility of leadership at their disposal, but may lead mistakenly to advance their own agenda. According to the prophets of God, God laments the gullibility and the blind submission of people to wicked religious leaders (Jeremiah 5:30-31; Ezekiel 13:19-21; Isaiah 9:14-16). Gullibility and blind submission are not commendable virtues. Are gullibility and submissiveness the very characteristics of the masses of Catholics whom the Vatican affectionately calls "the simple faithful" and heavily counts on to follow? One day I met in a market place an old woman who was about 70 years old. And we had a casual conversation on a bench for a few minutes. I asked her, "Are you a Christian?" She answered, "No I am not. I am not a Christian. I am a Catholic."

The inclination of the masses to idolatry also plays an important role in religion. The emotional enthusiasm and the personality cult which visibly appeared preceding and following the death of the pope John Paul II in April, 2005 are an example of this. This popular devotion and personality cult have been further inflamed by prominent political leaders of the world who made laudatory remarks in praise of the pope and attended his funeral. Their complimentary remarks may have been probably politically motivated in some or even many cases. There are over one billion Catholics today, many of whom will be pleased to hear such remarks. So great is the power of popular religion! The history of religions shows that religion and politics often joined hands and, as far as their leaders saw, benefited mutually.

The small voices of some theologians, historians and prophets have been drowned out by the tumultuous outbursts of the popular devotion and the mass media which are, so to speak, like the noises of huge tidal waves of the sea. The voices which sounded a different note, speaking truth, have been and are hardly audible and few seem to listen to them. Such appears to be the way things are in this world. Popularity, a large number of adherents and power are not necessarily a reliable index of the truth of a religion and an institutional church.

Traditionally the Roman Catholic Church has made a sharp divide between the Church and the world, between the spiritual and the temporal, and between the sacred and the profane. Is such dualism a teaching of the Scripture?

Although its doctrines and official theology often promote this divide, in reality the Roman Church has greatly benefited in terms of increased popularity and power from the way things are in this world. Revealed here is a contradiction that exists in the Catholic Church. There are more contradictions in the Church, and they will be examined in this book. This book is intended for both the general reader and the religious academic. It could also be used as Christian college and seminary textbook as well in the areas of theology and church history.

Finally, it is the writer's hope that the discussions in the book will serve in some small way as an aid for the readers to better comprehend the Christianity attested to in the Holy Scripture. He has endeavored to clarify the biblical concept of God and Christianity.

IV

THE ROMAN CATHOLIC CHURCH IN THE LAST 70 YEARS

THE ROMAN CATHOLIC CHURCH IS a unique religious phenomenon with a number of salient features: a pyramidal authoritarian structure under the sole rule of the pope who claims supremacy and infallibility as invested by God. It is an imperium with a centralized ecclesiastical government, with the pope at its apex who rules the Roman Catholic Church from its centre in Rome. Also it is a thoroughly ritualistic and sacramentalist religion which means to take care of the believer's spiritual life from birth to death. The Church claims to have received the power which reaches even to the world beyond this life after death. The Church has an exalted imposing hierarchy with different grades. This hierarchy controls the life of the Church and its individual members. In the Middle Ages the popes made claims to the political powers as well, claiming that these powers were endowed by God. The Roman Church is still prosperous and the number of its adherents is one half of the total Christian population in the world. A remarkable hypothetical theory has been put forward by church historians, theologians and sociologists that the Roman Catholic Church is not a true development from the Gospel of Jesus Christ testified in the New Testament, but it has historically developed largely after the model of the authoritarian administrative system and jurisprudence of the ancient Roman Empire. The scholars who presented this hypothesis are numerous and they include Adolf Harnack, Arthur Mirgeler, Charles Gore, Hans Kueng, Francois Houtart and Andre Rousseasu. Hans Kueng is a Catholic. These scholars named above are not frivolous persons, but are distinguished and respected scholars in their fields. They are convinced that their hypothesis is based on the sufficient evidences. We tentatively accept the hypothesis and will test if it can be substantiated by historical, biblical and theological data.

The present volume also discusses scandalously immoral aspects in the history of the popes, which are largely unknown to the public. This sinful history does not, in the writer's humble opinion, constitute only a very small part of the papal history.

In any case it has made a lasting impact on the development of the Roman Catholic Church and on the history of Western Europe.

Between 847 and 852 came one of the most remarkable of forgeries, the so – called Pseudo – Isidorian Decretals – purporting to be collected by Isidor Mercater. It consisted of the decisions of the Popes and the councils from Clement of Rome in the first century to Gregory II in the eighth, part genuine and part forged. The early popes therein claimed for themselves the supreme jurisdiction. Neither the papacy nor the bishops were subject to the secular control. It was used mightily for the furtherance of the papal claims. The age was uncritical. It passed immediately as genuine, and was not exposed until the Reformation awakened the historical study in the 16th century.

V

THE POPE'S TREATIES WITH BRUTAL DICTATORS

In 1933, AS I ALREADY noted, the Pope concluded a Concordat (treaty) with Hitler's Germany. Several years earlier (1929) the Vatican had signed a similar treaty called the Lateran Treaty with Benito Mussolini, the Fascist dictator of Italy. According to the terms of the Lateran Treaty, Roman Catholicism became the sole recognized religion in the country. Crucially, the Treaty acknowledged the right of the pope to impose within Italy the new Code of Canon Law. As I mentioned earlier, the Code of Canon Law is the body of internal law of the Catholic Church promulgated by the pope in 1917. It was designed to establish and maintain the pope's absolute power and unchallenged domination from the Roman centre over the Catholic Churches of the world.

Mussolini approved this Code of Canon Law. In return he demanded and received from the pope the guarantee that political action of the clergy and all those in religious orders would be prohibited and there would be no political and social Catholicism (article 43). Mussolini needed this to consolidate his absolute political dictatorship in Italy. This was virtually a mutual aid pact between Mussolini and the pope. It has been pointed out that there was affinity between this state dictatorship of Mussolini and the ecclesiastical dictatorship of the pope. The powerful democratic Catholic Popular Party which the Vatican had not supported and which was in many respects similar to the Catholic Centre Party in Germany was disbanded under mounting pressures, and its leader exiled.

Catholics were instructed by the Vatican to withdraw from politics as Catholics, leaving a political vacuum in which the Fascist regime was able to act freely. In the elections following the Lateran Treaty, priests throughout Italy were encouraged by the Vatican to support the Fascists, and the pope spoke of Mussolini as "a man sent by Providence".

Not surprisingly, Adolf Hitler, the future Nazi dictator praised the Lateran Treaty and hoped for an identical agreement for his future regime. A few days after the signing of the Lateran Treaty Hitler wrote an article for the newspaper Voelkisher Beobachter (People's Observer) on February 22, 1929 and said, "The fact that the Curia is now making its peace with Fascism shows that the Vatican trusts the new political realities far more than it did the former liberal democracy with which it could not come to terms". Turning to the German political situation, Hitler rebuked the (Catholic) Centre Party leadership for its stubborn attachment to democratic politics. "By truing to preach that democracy is still in the best interests of German politics, the Centre Party ... is placing itself in stark contradiction to the spirit of the treaty signed today by the Holy See." Hitler also said, "The fact that the Catholic Church has come to an agreement with Fascist Italy ... proves beyond doubt that the Fascist world of ideas is closer to Christianity than those of Jewish liberalism or even atheistic Marxism." As the Fascism of Mussolini and the Nazism of Hitler's Germany were similar ideologies, it was natural that the two dictators became allies during the Second World War. In 1933 the Vatican signed *the Reich Concordat* with Hitler's Germany, which was in practical purposes a mutual aid pact between the two dictators, namely the pope and Hitler, at the sacrifice of the well-being, integrity and honour of the Catholic Church in Germany. I will elaborate this point.

Hitler feared the resistance and opposition of political Christianity, whether Catholic or Protestant, to his National Socialism (Nazism), and was determined to find a way to neutralize the church, as far as its political influence was concerned. His fear came from his knowledge of the historical precedent of Catholic reaction to Bismarck's Kulturkampf (culture struggle). Otto von Bismarck (1815-98) was the first chancellor of the modern German Empire, and Kulturkampf refers to the conflict between the German imperial government and the Roman Catholic Church in the 1870s and 1880s chiefly over the control of educational and ecclesiastical appointments. Bismarck did not win in the bitter conflict. In a letter (1929) to a Catholic Nazi Father Magnus Goett, Hitler said, "I always and under all circumstances take it to be a misfortune when religion, regardless in which form, is joined to political parties." He also accused the Catholic Centre Party of waging a bitter conflict against the national idea since the end of the First World War.

As it happened, bolstered by the strength of the Catholic Centre Party, the Catholic Church in Germany saw an unprecedented growth and expansion, not only in religious but also in cultural and political terms. The Catholic population in Germany was about 23 million by 1930, about 35 percent of the nation. Catholic opposition to Hitler's National Socialism (Nazism) was strong and sustained in the press and from the pulpits. I give a few examples. In these accounts the writer is entirely indebted to John Cornwell's *Hitler's Pope* (1999). A Catholic Journalist Walter Dirks, writing in the August 1931 edition of the journal *Die Arbeit* (Labour), described the Catholic reaction to Nazism as "open warfare", and asserted that the ideology of Nazism "stood in blatant explicit contrast to the Church". In the spring of 1931, the Catholic Reichstag (Parliament) representative Karl Trossmann published a book entitled *Hitler and Rome* in which he described the National Socialists as a "brutal party that would do away with all the rights of the people." He said that Hitler was dragging Germany into a new war, a war that "would only end more disastrously than the last war." The Catholic author Alfons Wild also published a widely distributed essay entitled "Hitler and Catholicism" in which he declared that "Hitler's view of the world is not Christianity but the message of race, a message that does not proclaim peace and justice but rather violence and hate."

Meanwhile, two Catholic journalists, Frita Gerlich and Ingbert Naab, co-authored an article for the Munich-based journal Der Gerade Weg (The Straight Path), denouncing National Socialism. In the issue dated July 21, 1932 the writers said that "National Socialism means enmity with neighbouring countries, despotism in internal affairs, civil war and international war. National Socialism means lies, hatred, fratricide and unbounded misery. Adolf Hitler preaches the law of lies. You who have fallen victim to the deception of one obsessed with despotism, wake up!"

Thus, German Catholic journalists and writers accurately perceived the true nature of Hitler's Nazism and correctly predicted its consequences. Not only the journalists and writers, but average thinking Catholics also shared their view, according to Cornwell.

Likewise the Roman bishops also recognized the unchristian character of Nazism. The Catholic bishop's office in Mainz drew attention to the "Hitler Party's policy of racial hatred" and pointed out the fact that "the religious and educational policy of National Socialism is inconsistent with Catholic Christianity." Yet the Catholic bishops failed to produce a single unanimous document when they gathered for conference in the late autumn 1930. Instead, the president of the bishop's conference made a New Year statement, warning the Catholic Church in Germany against political extremism and the wickedness of racism.

In February 1931, the Bavarian bishops made a more specific directive for the clergy in their region. They said, "As guardians of the true teaching of faith and morals, the bishops must warn against National Socialism. So long and so far as it proclaims cultural and political options that are incompatible with Catholic teachings." The following month, the German Catholic archbishops stated in the clearest terms that National Socialism and Catholicism were incompatible, and repeated the key sentence of the Bavarian bishops' letter. Thus, there was a strong and united front of the Catholic Church in Germany against Hitler's National Socialism in 1931.

Then, how is it that Catholic antagonism to Nazism failed to materialize in the form of the confrontation Hitler greatly feared? The answer is that the Vatican intervened with superior authority to override the opposition of the German Catholic Church to Nazism. Why did the Vatican do that? Because the Vatican shrewdly perceived that having a concordat with Hitler's regime was in the best interest of reinforcing and keeping secure the pope's absolute centrist domination of the Catholic Church in Germany and elsewhere. All other considerations were secondary. The pope's lust for power and callous egotism were the main motive.

This is not the first time that the Vatican betrayed the high cause it is supposed to stand for. We have seen it in the Vatican's Lateran Treaty with the Fascist dictator Mussolini of Italy in 1929 as well. The Catholic historian Cornwell said, "The Holy See for centuries had been in the habit of signing treaties with monarchs and governments inimical to its beliefs and values." One will get a moral shock or one may not believe it. But there are almost innumerable cases of the "Holy" See's very unholy behavior in church history. Here I quote again the noteworthy remark of the Catholic Archbishop Luigi Puecher-Passavalli of Italy, "The personnel of the Pontifical Curia have produced in me an unconquerable conviction that never, never to the very end of the world, will they consent to renounce Temporal Power ... They will utilize every means (at one time public at another secret, at one time more violent at another less so) to repossess themselves of the Power at any and every price. Not Religion, not Piety, not Christianity, not Theology is the proper interest of the members of the Pontifical Curia, but the political advantage of political institution." This remark is, in our view, true not only of the members of the Pontifical Curia but also of the pope himself. This Italian archbishop had a long acquaintance with the Pope.

CHAPTER

VI

THE POPE'S CALLOUS EGOTISM

THE POPE'S CALLOUS EGOTISM WAS already shown, for instance, in its preoccupation with preserving Rome safe from the Allied bombing during the Second World War although there were other urgent matters which called for the Vatican's immediate attention and action. This was so much the case that it drew a British diplomat's sharp rebuke.

In the early 1930s the German Catholic Church, with its 23 million faithfuls, was a powerful independent constituency, together with the Catholic hierarchy and the Catholic Centre Party. The German Chancellor Hitler feared the opposition from the Roman Church united as a political force. As Hitler did not want to provoke a new *Kulturkampf* with the Catholic Church he avoided directly taking on the bishops. But something had to be done to neutralize them, and here the Vatican came to Hitler's aid, with its own ambitious project and goals. But as the pope Pius XI was in poor health, it was the Cardinal Secretary of State Eugenio Pacelli who conducted in the name of the pope the successful negotiation of the Reich Concordat with Hitler. This is the reason why Pacelli who took the papal office after Pius XI's death came to be called "Hitler's Pope" by Cornwell.

The basic requirement of the treaty from Hitler's point of view was the voluntary withdrawal of the clergy from the political and social action and the disbanding of the Catholic Centre Party in exchange for guaranteeing the religious rights of the Catholics. But before its disbanding the Party had to give legal force to the passing of the Enabling Act in the Reichstag (Parliament) that would grant Hitler the constitutional powers of dictatorship. When these requirements from Hitler were made known, the Catholic bishops vehemently rejected them. By 1933 in which the Concordat with Hitler's regime was signed and ratified, the brutal and despotic nature of the regime, its unChrichtian ideology and hatred, anti-Semitism and paganism were already apparent for all to see. This is why the German Catholic Church strongly opposed the Concordat with the Nazi regime.

To make a long story short, both the German Catholic bishops and the Centre Party capitulated to the will of the Vatican. Under the increasing pressure of the Vatican the bishops revoked their opposition to Hitler's National Socialism and endorsed the Concordat. The Catholic Centre Party also was compelled to support the Enabling Act at the critical parliamentary vote, and a few months afterwards disbanded. Thus the sole surviving democratic party worth the name in Germany disappeared.

Thus, Hitler got everything he demanded. The treaty called "the Reich Concordat" was formally signed in the Vatican on July 20, 1933. For its part, the Vatican too obtained what it valued most highly and desired most, the right to impose the Code of Canon Law on the Catholic Church in Germany. Article 31 on the Concordat acknowledged the Holy See's right to control and coerce Catholic clergy in Germany with efficient sanctions through the Canon Law. Thus, the two dictators, the one political and the other ecclesiastical, got what they wanted at the expense of the integrity, honour and wellbeing of the German Catholic Church. There was a remarkable similarity between this authoritarian state of Hitler and the authoritarian church of the pope. During the negotiations with Hitler for the treaty the Vatican ignored the protests, demands and hopes of the German bishops and clergy. The Vatican's main concern was to reinforce the already formidable central power of the pope at the expense of all other matters. The Concordat was a triumph for canon law and a victory for the papacy. Cornwell made this comment regarding the Concordat, " ...A bid for unprecedented papal power ... had drawn the Catholic Church into complicity with the darkest forces of the era." This complicity helped Hitler. Along with other factors, it emboldened Hitler to make an adventure of starting a war which led to the Second World War. Thus the Vatican made some contribution to the outbreak of the War. There is no evidence that the Vatican prudently considered the consequences of the Concordat with Hitler. Its greatest concern was with advancing the pope's absolute power exercised from the Roman centre, including the pope's exclusive right to nominate the bishops of his choice. Human rights and social ethics were not matters of concern to the Vatican. Here we recall a remarkable statement noted earlier made by Cardinal Eugene Tisserant, "I fear that history will reproach the Holy See for having practiced a policy of selfish convenience and little else."

Cornwell plausibly argues that if there had been no Concordat with Hitler's regime, the German Catholic Church which was powerful and united against Hitler's National Socialism would have protested, refused to cooperate and resisted Hitler's policy, and history might have been different. Cornwell gives an account of a number of significant and even successful resistances and demonstrations before the Concordat, which compelled the Nazi authorities to retreat. "Had these protests been repeated and extended in a multiplicity of local instances across Germany, from 1933 onwards, the history of the Nazi regime might have taken a different course." The Holocaust might not have taken place, and the outbreak of the War might have been put off or even avoided. Then the history of Europe and of the world would have been very different.

After the Concordat, however, there were no more protests, demonstrations, or resistance. The German Catholic Church was demoralized and paralyzed under the tight control by the Vatican and the Nazi regime. The Church was sacrificed for the sake of establishing the centrist papal power.

The collapse of the once great Centre Party drove Catholics in ever greater numbers into the bosom of National Socialism. In other words they became Nazis themselves. The conversion of Catholics to the National Socialists, at first a trickle, now became "a great river", in the words of Cornwell. The current pope Benedict XVI too (who was crowned in April, 2005 after the death of the Pope John Paul II) joined as a youth the Hitler's youth organization (Hitler Jugend) in 1941. In domestic politics, the Reich Concordat integrated the Catholics and their bishops into the Nazi system. In foreign politics, it bestowed on the Nazi dictator the first international recognition.

Here I will examine the actions of the Vatican during the years of the World War II and in the years preceding and following the war, and also on the behaviour of the successors of Pope John XXIII after the Second Vatican Council. I take this focus because I think that their actions and behaviours reveal the real nature of the papacy and what the Roman popes seek after most. This will, in turn, throw light on the Roman Church and give us some insight into the religion with the name of Roman Catholicism. The account which follows is based on John Cornwell's historical work. *Hitler's Pope-the Secret History of Puis XII (1999)*. Cornwell was Senior Research Fellow at Jesus College, Cambridge, England; he is now in the department of history and philosophy of science at Cambridge University. He is an award-winning journalist and author. He authored three highly regarded books, two of which are on popes. He has written on Catholic issues for many publications around the world. His *Hitler's Pope* was an acclaimed best seller on the *New York Times*. Cornwell appears to be a Roman Catholic. *Hitler's Pope* is the previously untold story of Eugenio Pacelli, pope Pius XII (1939-58), who was arguably the most powerful and dangerous pope in modern history. Cornwell wrote *Hitler's Pope* drawing on research from secret Vatican and Jesuit archives made available to him.

The main point of Cornwell's thesis in this book is that the Vatican prompted events in the 1920s and 30s which helped Adolf Hitler's rise to power unopposed. It reveals the Vaticans egoistic ambitions to advance the pope's autocratic power over the entire Catholic Church, and thereby unintentionally contributed to the outbreak of the World War II. The Vatican struck a Concord with Hitler which gave him the first international recognition and also helped him move swiftly to a legal dictatorship while neutralizing the potential of Germany's 23 million Catholics (34 million after the Anschluss with Austria) to protest and resist. Not only that, but according to Cornwell, much earlier the Vatican was also responsible for a treaty with Serbia which contributed to the rising tensions that led to the World War I. Thus the Vatican's main concern was with advancing the papal power over the Roman Church not only in Germany but throughout the world, regardless of its consequences for world peace, the well-being of peoples, and the interests of the German Catholic Church which was the most powerful in the world. What is apparent is the lust for power and "callous egotism" of the pope.

Hitler's Pope gives a portrait of pope Pius XII, who took office in 1939 on the eve of the Second World War and remained in office until his death in 1958, as a narcissistic, power hungry manipulator who was prepared to lie, appease and collaborate with the Nazi dictator in order to accomplish his ecclesiastical program, all to protect and reinforce the absolute power of the papacy. *The Washington Post*, in its book review, said that Hitler's Pope "redefines the entire history of the 20ᵗʰ century." *The New York Times* Book Review also said, "Explosive … (Cornwell) makes a case in Hitler's Pope that is very difficult to refute." Cornwell's account is difficult to refute because it is well-documented.

The pope's egotism was also revealed in the fact that throughout the war years Pius XII was obsessed with one issue above all others, namely the preservation of Rome from aerial bombardment by the Allied air forces. He feared that Allied bombers would destroy Rome and the Vatican as they did other cities in Europe. So he repeatedly requested that Rome be exempted and his efforts paid off. Critics pointed out that the pope was guilty of a double standard, and thought that he was perhaps afraid of being bombed in the Vatican.

Critics also pointed out that while being obsessed with the safety of Rome and the Vatican and making ceaseless attempts to protect Rome from the Allied bombing, the pope did practically nothing about the Holocaust (mass murders of Jews by the Nazis), or about the Catholic Croatians' campaign of terror and extermination against two million Serb Orthodox Christians (an act of "ethnic cleansing" before the term came into vogue) during the war years. The Croatian Catholics massacred one fourth of the two million Serbs between 1941 and 1945. Unlike the Nazi atrocities the Croatian atrocities are not widely known.

Regarding the pope's preoccupation with preventing the bombing of Rome, Francis D' Arcy Osborne, the British minister at the Holy See, resident in the Vatican at the time, confided in his diary on December 13, 1942. "The more I think of it, the more I am revolted by Hitler's massacre of the Jewish race on the one hand, and, on the other, the Vatican's apparently exclusive preoccupation with the … possibilities of the bombardment of Rome." A few days later, he wrote to the Cardinal Secretary of State (of the Vatican) that the Vatican "instead of thinking of nothing but the bombing of Rome should consider their duties in respect of the unprecedented crime against humanity of Hitler's campaign of extermination of Jews. "Osborne's diary was quoted by Owen Chadwick, in *Britain and the Vatican during the Second World War* (Cambridge, 1989). Throughout the period, urgent pleas had been coming to the Vatican for help from Jewish communities and organizations of the world. Osborne being the British minister of the Holy See was the main channel through whom the pope conducted the negotiation with Allies about preserving Rome from the aerial bombardment. The secretary of State of the Vatican is the second in rank and power to the pope. The Vatican, including the pope, was taught a moral lesson by a British diplomat. This is a shame of maximum magnitude for the Vatican, especially for the pope who claims to be the Vicar of Christ and the infallible teacher of faith and morals.

VII

THE SECOND VATICAN COUNCIL AND THE STALLED REFORM OF THE CATHOLIC CHURCH

WE HAVE SEEN THAT AFTER a long historical process the Popes' sole rule of the Catholic Church, rigidly centralized, bureaucratized and clericalized, was finally established, and continued to exist until the middle of the 20th century.

Then something unexpected happened. Pope John XXIII (1958-63), the son of an Italian peasant farmer, called the Second Vatican Council in 1959 with a view to pastoral renewal and the promotion of Christian unity. The pope attributed the calling of the historic council to a sudden inspiration of the Holy Spirit. He proclaimed the principle of "aggiornamento," that the Church should develop and change with society and history. He brought winds of change to the Vatican and the Roman Church, relaxing the stiffness of the centralized hierarchical power structure. This was an unprecedented, sudden development in the history of the papacy and of the Roman Catholic Church. So a large segment of Catholics within the Church hailed it with excitement, and the whole Christian world watched the development in surprise and high expectation.

The Council (1962-1965) made many decisions that gave rise to historic changes – in liturgy and biblical studies, dialogue with the Protestant and Orthodox Churches, and a declaration on religious freedom. But the single most important decision for change was the call for "collegiality", a code word for more democracy in the Roman Church and power sharing between the pope and the bishops. This was to put an end to the one-man rule of the Catholic Church of the world, to decentralize and deabsolutize the papacy and to end the ideology of papal power which was brought in by the First Vatican Council (1869-1870) and pursued ever since. Also the Council restored the biblical concept of the church as the people of God and placed it in tension with the organizational and juridical concept which has been the dominant concept in the Roman Church.

Not surprisingly, there was die-hard resistance and objection to the church reform from the traditionalists during and after the Council. Then very regrettably, John XXIII died during the Council before the decisions of the Council were implemented and the reform was entrenched. After John's death his successors, Paul VI and John Paul II, the curia and other traditionalist forces quickly overpowered the reform advocates, and returned the Roman Church to its old state. Their main objection was to "collegiality", and so the Roman Catholic Church headed back toward the old days. The new popes disagreed with their predecessor John XXIII on the issue of collegiality and totally ignored him. Many Catholics are perhaps unaware that there was a gigantic struggle in the Church over the reform of the Church and that the struggle is still on-going in some ways.

Among the major historic decisions made by the Council was the decision to set up the "Synod of Bishops". The Synod was meant to be the chief structural means of change. However, the papacy has been and still is the greatest obstacle to change and to the union of the Christian churches. Pope Paul VI himself has several times admitted that the papacy, under the present aspect, is a major obstacle to the union of the Churches.

Apparently here is a self-contradiction of the Roman Church. However, the Catholic Church has managed to avoid the self-contradiction by the usual claim that only the Roman Catholic Church headed by the pope who is the successor of Peter and the Vicar of Christ on earth is "the Church." We feel that this is an arrogance and pretension on the part of the Catholic Church. The arrogance appears even more remarkable when we consider the magnitude of corruption and deceit of this official Catholic Church as manifested in the successive employment of "forgeries"; "it has followed the Machiavellian practice of other kingdoms, condoning torture and assassination" (Garry Wills); sales of Indulgences, of ecclesiastical offices, and of God's grace and blessing in the Middle Ages. Renaissance popes who, while imposing celibacy on the priests with an iron hand, "lived in monstrous luxury, unbridled sensuality and uninhibited vice" (Hans Kueng); popes' seemingly insatiable lust for power; unceasing power struggles within and without the church; maneuvers; manipulative interpretations of the Bible to aggrandize the Roman Church and to exalt and empower the priestly caste; often being an enemy of the human rights, freedom and social justice; a papal tribunal called the Inquisition which existed for five centuries in Europe and burned alive to death many thousands of "heretics" and witches; the so-called crusades that slaughtered hundreds of thousands of Christians for not submitting to the papal authority and the papal church; seeking and establishing the autocratic power structure of the papacy at the expense of justice and humanity, of the peace of the world, of the wellbeing of people, and of the integrity and well-being of regional churches; the signing of treaties with brutal dictators for questionable mutual benefit; the would-be Vicar of Christ that kept silence in the face of the Nazi Holocaust of six million Jews, and his successors who disregard it and even defend him; the use of the name of Christ and religion to advance the interests of the papacy; and so on and on.

These historical facts indicate an astonishing moral and spiritual degeneration. It is unbelievable that the living Vicar of Christ and the Church founded by Christ and allegedly having been supernaturally protected by God went down to such a low state. The Roman Church itself has been the greatest victim of the popes' love of power across many centuries. The Roman Catholic Church is comparable to a large passenger ship that has been seized by a band of pirate on the high sea and has been forced to proceed in an altered wrong direction. We have used this analogy earlier.

VIII

THE POPE'S CLAIM TO THE PRIMACY

THE ROMAN CATHOLIC CHURCH CLAIMS that it was founded by Christ and is endowed with authority which is not less than divine. Unlike the church in the New Testament which is conceived primarily as the people of God, this authoritarian church has an ecclesiastical government run by the clerical hierarchy. The pope who is at the top of this hierarchy is held to have been divinely appointed, and he delegates authority to lower ranks of the clergy. So every parish priest shares in the authority of the Church, limited in its exercise by higher ranks of the hierarchy. It is claimed that "the Roman Pontiff has full and supreme jurisdiction over the universal Church," and submission to the Church headed by the pope is demanded of every Catholic. Catholics are also required to believe what is taught "on the authority of the Church". This dual demand, perhaps more than anything else, clearly reveals the authoritarian character of the Roman Catholic Church. It also shows unmistakably, in our view, the contrast between the two concepts of the church, namely, the Catholic and the biblical concept.

The pope's claim to authority which is no less than divine is chiefly based on a peculiar interpretation of Christ's saying to Peter recorded in Matthew 16:18-9. Christ said: *I say to you that you are Peter, and upon this rock I will build my church; and the gates of Hades shall not overcome it. I will give you the keys of heaven; and whatever you shall bind on earth will be bound in heaven, and whatever you shall loose on earth will be loosed in heaven.*

On these words the Roman Church bases its threefold claim that to Peter was given the first place among the apostles and indeed authority over them; that to Peter was given the power to forgive sin or to retain it, and so to open or close the gates of heaven to other men; and that to Peter was also given the power to transmit these powers to the man he is pleased to appoint as his successor. It is further claimed that the bishop of Rome, namely the pope, is the successor of Peter; therefore whatever powers were given to Peter have been passed on to the pope. The pope is in principle able to choose his successor if he wills, but under the current system, a new pope is elected by the College of Cardinals. The dogma of papal infallibility is also based on inference from the same words of Jesus in Matthew 16:18-19. This text has been invoked to claim the supremacy of the bishop of Rome (the pope) over all other bishops and over the Christian churches throughout the world.

It is intriguing to see how the above-mentioned stupendous claims are deduced from Matthew 16:18-19. It is by an unusual imagination and ingenious inference. It will be difficult or even impossible for an ordinary person to read in Matthew 16:18-19 what the Roman Church reads into it. The text does not plainly say those things the pope of Rome claims; certainly there is nothing in the text which refers to the Roman Church or the bishop of Rome.

The pope's claim was ignored until the 5th century even in the West, let alone in the East. Gradually, however, the papal claim to primacy came to be generally recognized in the West, if not in the East. Papal primacy was afterwards interpreted as the supremacy of the pope, and the pope claimed to be "the vicar of Christ" on earth. In *The Catechism of the Catholic Church*, we read:

For the Roman Pontiff, by reason of his office as Vicar of Christ ... has full, supreme, and universal power over the whole Church, a power which he can always exercise unhindered.

<No. 9882>

But the Catholic interpretation of Matt. 16:18-19 and the papal claims have serious difficulties. There is no biblical and historical evidence that the apostle Peter claimed such powers for himself or exercised them. There is rather contrary evidence. This means that the pope of Rome makes claim to powers which Peter himself did not make. Neither in the two epistles of Peter nor in the writings of the Church Fathers of the second and the third century is there a reference along the line that Peter claimed and actually exercised a special power beyond the commonly shared power of the apostles.

As Matthew 16:18-19 does not say in plain words that Jesus invested Peter with the above-mentioned threefold power and infallibility, it is apparent that the Roman Church obtained its interpretation by means of stretching the meaning of the text. Here we present the thesis that if one stretches the meaning of a biblical text in the manner the Catholic Church does, he can prove by the Bible almost any strange idea he happens to like. Such a method will distort the meaning of the biblical text. I remind the reader that I am not saying that the monarchical papacy of the Roman Catholic Church developed and was established based on its interpretation of Matthew 16:18-9 (and a few other biblical texts). This is not the case. The monarchical papacy was first established through the determined effort and struggles of the ambitious bishops of Rome, under the influence of the legalistic spirit of the ancient Romans and after the model of the Roman Empire. The papalist interpretation of the biblical texts and the elaborate argument were formulated by theologians many centuries later to provide a biblical and theological basis for what already existed, and to solidify it. The pope and the curia in the Middle Ages had no due respect for, nor practical concern with, the Holy Scripture and theology.

The Orthodox Church and the Anglican Church as well as the Protestant Churches do not accept the papalist interpretation of

Matthew 16:18, and they reject the dogma of papal primacy. They hold that the Roman interpretation is unjustified and the papal claim is unfounded. They also point out that the papal claim to primacy is the major reason that the Church of Jesus Christ remains divided despite the earnest plea of the Lord Jesus for unity (John 17:11, 21-22; 10:16). To this, Catholic theologians loyal to the pope invoke another dogma of the Roman Church, namely, the dogma of the Church's teaching authority (the so-called magisterium), and argue roughly as follows: The Catholic Church is the depository of the supernatural salvific truth of God. The Catholic Church alone, specifically the pope alone, has received the authority of infallibly interpreting and teaching the Bible. Therefore the non-Catholic Churches have no right to put forward an interpretation of the Bible which differs from what the Roman Church proclaims to be the true one.

Here an inevitable question is: On what ground does the teaching authority of the Catholic Church assert that it is divinely invested with the authority of infallibly interpreting the Bible, in the present case, Matthew 16:18? To answer this question it is claimed that the Roman Church's infallible teaching authority is justified by Matthew 16:18, and it is this very authority which infallibly interprets Matthew 16:18.

This is a typical circular argument. If there is a logic in this argument at all, it is good only within the closed circle. Outside the circle, it loses force and proves nothing. The closed circle also refers to the huge edifice of Roman Catholicism. Matt. 16:18, thus interpreted, is one of the major pillars supporting the grand edifice of the Roman Church.

Peter's eminence among the apostles is admitted. but Peter was eminent in a representative way, rather than in a leadership capacity. We can offer biblical evidence which, in our view, refute the papalist assertion of Peter's primacy.

a. The leading position was seemingly held by James, the brother of our Lord, in the early years of the Church. Consider the Council at Jerusalem which is recorded in the fifteenth chapter of Acts, especially verses 13 to 29.

b. Regardless of who was the leader, the Council's decision was not one leader's authoritative action. The decision and its implementation were the Council's collegial action. What we see here is the "collegiality" of the apostles rather than the sole dictatorship like the monarchical papacy of the Roman Church.

c. The apostles as a body in Jerusalem sent Peter and John to Samaria on a mission (Acts: 14-17).

d. Paul withstood Peter to the face in the presence of others when he found Peter's action to be against the principle of the Gospel (Galatians 2:1-14).

e. There was a rough division of the mission field among the apostles. Peter was the apostle to the Jews while Paul was to the Gentiles (Galatians 2:6-9). Peter was not an overall supervisor.

f. The circumcised believers (Jewish Christians) criticized Peter for the latter's having eaten with the Gentile Christians (Acts 11:1-3).

I would like to elaborate on a, b, c and d. in the days of the apostles, it appears that the prominent leader was James, the brother of Jesus, rather than Peter. The story in Acts 15 about the historic Council of the apostles and the elders who gathered to discuss a vitally important theological issue shows this. In the meeting of the Council Peter made an important contribution, but it was James who made the final conclusive speech and his proposal was adopted as a whole and implemented. It appears that James acted as the chairman at the Council. Elsewhere the apostle Paul says that James, Peter and John were "reputed to be pillars" of the Jerusalem church (Galatians 2:9). Paul also gives an interesting account about a significant incident. He says that he rebuked Peter in the presence of people for Peter's hypocrisy and wrong action (Galatians 2:1). If Peter were recognized as the supreme leader set apart by Christ from other apostles as the Roman Church asserts, it is improbable that Paul would dare to rebuke Peter in the presence of people. Furthermore, the way Peter acted in the incident is not that of an undisputed leader.

Acts 8:14 says, "Now when the apostles in Jerusalem heard that Samaria had received the word of God, they sent there Peter and John, who came down and prayed for them, that they might receive the Holy Spirit." Obviously the apostles in Jerusalem consulted on the matter and acted as a body, and sent Peter and John on a mission. Here there is no indication that Peter was recognized by the apostles as the undisputed leader invested with special authority and status by Christ as Rome asserts. There are a few more biblical passages which seem to indicate that it was James, rather than Peter, who was regarded as the leading personality (Acts 21:18, 12:17). In the two epistles attributed to Peter, Peter does not say anything which suggests his special position and authority. Rather he speaks as one of many (elders). Also in neither of the two epistles does the word "church" appears. Time and again Peter mentions the prophets of God with high respect; this line of thought is not congruous with the ecclesiastic sacerdotal religion which Roman Catholicism is. Further, sadly for the Roman Church, Peter taught the doctrine of the priesthood of all believers (I Peter 2:9). This doctrine undermines any priestly institution set up in the Christian Church.

Who is Peter? Peter is asserted to be the head of the apostolic college; and the pope of Rome claims to be Peter's successor. Based on Jesus' saying to Peter, "The gates of hell shall not overcome the church," it is claimed that the Church of Rome is under the supernatural protection of God. Thus the prestige of the Roman Church is greatly increased. But Peter said things which would damage the claimed prestige and authority of the Church. For example, Peter said:

> For it is time for the judgement (of God) to begin with the house of God; if it begins with us first, what will be the outcome for those who do not obey the gospel of God? (1 Peter 4:17) "The house of God" refers to the church.

The apostles and the early church believed that Christ's second coming in glory and God's judgment of the world were impending. They did not expect that there would be a long period of the Church on earth that would last for thousands years. Peter warned that God's judgment would "begin with the house of God". This warning contradicts the pretentious claims of the Roman Church that as the Mystical Body of Christ and the extended and continued Incarnation of Christ, the Catholic Church is vested with the authority which is not less than divine, and is infallible and incorruptible, and that the Roman Church is the Kingdom of God on earth and as such is free from the relativity and ambiguity of history. It is a common teaching of the Old and the New Testament that God will judge His own people first (Jeremiah 7:12-15, 25:29; Ezekiel 9:6; Amos 3:2; Isaiah 10:12; I Peter 4:17). In the New Testament the church is primarily the people of God, called to modesty and lowliness. Peter thinks of the church as the people of God (2:9-10). The people of God are those who have been chosen and called by God and who are now pilgrims and exiles in the world (1:1-3, 2:11). For Peter, the church is the flock of God (5:2) and Christ is the Chief Shepherd (5:4). Peter says that the ministers of the church are shepherds of the sheep. Jesus himself called his followers the "little flock" (Luke 12:32) of which he was the Shepherd. He said that there were "other sheep" besides and he will bring them so that they become one flock with one Shepherd (John 10:16). The image of the church as sheep is anything but self-exalting and authoritarian. It is also worth noting that the church is differentiated from the ministers of the church in the Acts of the Apostles (15:4, 22, 14:23 and 20:28). The essential component of church is the people, rather than the clergy.

To sum up, for Peter the church is the chosen people, pilgrims in the world and the flock of God. The humble and lowly image of the church of God which is conveyed here is just the contrary of the grandiose triumpalistic image of the church as conceived by the Roman Catholic Church. Yet the pope of Rome claims that he is the successor of Peter. In the New Testament there is another figure of speech about the church, namely, that the church is the bride of

Christ. To think of the humble people of God who call on the name of the Lord Jesus Christ, as "the bride of Christ" makes sense. To think of the authoritarian self-exalting hierarchical church as the bride of Christ is contrary to the New Testament depiction. We continue our study of the words Jesus said to Peter as recorded in Matthew's gospel:

> I will give you the keys of the kingdom of heaven; whatever you bind on earth will be bound in heaven, and whatever you loose on earth will be loosed in heaven.
>
> <Matthew 16:19>

How are these words to be interpreted? If they are interpreted literally, such an interpretation creates enormous difficulty. It is to be borne in mind that Jesus used many parables, metaphors and symbolical words in his teaching.

Consider another saying of Jesus to Peter which is recorded in the same chapter of Matthew.

> "Out of my sight, Satan! You are a stumbling block to me, you do not have in mind the things of God, but the things of men."
>
> <Matthew 16:23>

Jesus said this when Peter rebuked him for having foretold that he (Jesus) would suffer in Jerusalem and be killed. If this saying is taken literally, Peter is now "Satan", the devil. We notice that Jesus said exactly the same thing to the devil when the latter tempted Jesus to worship him (Matthew 4:8-10). "Out of my sight, Satan", said Jesus. There is nothing strange in Jesus calling the evil tempter "Satan", but to call Peter his disciple "Satan" is another matter. Is it conceivable that Jesus builds his Church on "Satan" and gives him the keys of the kingdom of heaven? The literal interpretation of Jesus' saying to Peter creates great difficulty. If we understand these words as symbolical or figurative sayings, the difficulty will be lessened greatly. One may interpret that when Jesus said these harsh words to

Peter, he (Jesus) was addressing whatever in Peter has been perversely influenced by the prince of evil. Then Peter is not literally Satan. The Catholic doctrines of the church, the sacrament and the papacy were formulated by way of literal interpretation of a few biblical passages and also by arbitrary stretching of the meaning of the words.

"Binding" and "loosing" were idiomatic expressions in rabbinical Judaism to indicate the proclamation of rulings either forbidding or permitting various kinds of activity. The words "binding" and "loosing" are not to be taken literally.

There is another noteworthy problem. It is the fact that this saying of Christ recorded in Matthew 16:18-19 is not found in the gospels of Mark, Luke and John, but in Matthew only. Not only so with the exception of Matthew 16:18 and Matthew 18:17, the word "church" does not appear in the gospels. This surprising fact calls for an explanation. The fact that the parallel passage is missing in Mark's gospel and that Mark does not make a single reference to the church is remarkable. It is remarkable especially because Mark was a close associate of the apostle Peter, so close that Peter called Mark "my son" (I Peter 5:13). Mark's gospel is believed to depend mainly on the sources that derived from Peter.

Even if we allow that Matthew 16:18-19 is an authentic saying of Christ, that Peter was given primacy and authority over the other apostles and that Peter alone received the keys of heaven as the Roman Church asserts, it does not follow that the Roman pope's claim to primacy as Peter's successor is legitimate. For there is a crucial point to consider. The papal claim stands or falls with the truth or otherwise of the assertions that whatever were the powers given to Peter, he was empowered to transmit them to his successor, and that the bishop of Rome, among a number of bishops, became Peter's sole successor. Regarding the transmission of Peter's office and power to the bishop of Rome (later the pope), a Scottish theologian made a decades-long investigation and wrote, "For this assertion there is nothing that can be called evidence" (C. Anderson Scott: Romanism and the Gospel (1937), p. 188). Many other theologians and church historians have reached the same conclusion. We could say that there is a consensus about this question among reliable scholars. Only some loyal Catholic scholars disagree. We suspect that even some of the Catholic scholars, if they are good scholars, waver in their minds. However, the fact is that no scholars, whether Catholic or not, has produced so far any solid historical or biblical evidence to support the papal claim to primacy.

There have been numerous forged documents to legitimize the monarchical papacy and its power. But their being forgeries was later detected by historians. For example, a second-century forgery which gives the earliest list of the bishops of Rome is a papalist attempt to produce a false evidence of Peter's episcopate in Rome. The attempt failed because historians have uncovered that it was a forgery. As we have already noted, forged documents appeared again and again in the history of the Roman Church, mostly to reinforce the papal power. The papal curia used these forgeries and they were quite effective in attaining its objective. We think that if the popes had not used these forgeries, the Roman papacy would be different from what it is today. Also it is to be pointed out that some of the old forgeries are still being used in unnoticeable ways. Theologians have noted them specifically. We have already dealt with this question. Yet the Vatican does not appear to be embarrassed by this and simply ignores it. This is a bizarre, incredible phenomenon. Do they have a right conscience? This writer finds it hard to expel the impression that "truth" is a scarce commodity in the catalogue of the claims and announcements made by the popes of Rome since the Middle Ages. The Catechism of the Catholic Church which was approved and ordered to be published by the pope John Paul II in 1992 gave the definition of sin as follows, "Sin is an offence against reason, truth, and right conscience" (No. 1849). If considered according to this definition of sin, the papacy is practically an institution of sin. Garry Wills, a Catholic historian, discusses the papal sin in his book *"Papal Sin"* (2000) and calls the institution of the papacy "structures of deceit". He wrote, "The truth, we are told, will make us free. It is time to free Catholics, lay as well as clerical, from the pressures of deceit, the quieter corruptions of intellectual betrayal" (from the Introduction). The writer feels that the history of the papacy is, in a sense, one long story of a gigantic fraud which unfolded over a period of some 16 centuries.

Regarding "the forgeries", the Catholic theologian Hans Kueng writes:

> *"All these forgeries are not curiosities of the time, as papal historians well-disposed toward the pope want to make out, but have had an abiding impact on the history of the church. The forgeries, most of which were subsequently legitimized by the pope, still appear in the Codex Iuris Canonici revised under the supervision of the curia and promulgated in 1983 by John Paul II."*

I have quoted this earlier. The Codex Iuris Cananonici (Latin, the Code of Canon Law) is a vast complex legal system which has played a vital role in maintaining the pope's centralized control of the Roman Catholic Church throughout the world. Such a canon law did not exist in the apostolic church and in the churches of early centuries.

Regarding the Catholic doctrine of the Apostolic Succession, I point out that in the New Testament the apostle is not an office holder, but a first-hand witness to Christ, his words, deeds, death and resurrection. Being irreplaceable and unique, the apostolate cannot be transmitted to or succeeded to by subsequent generations. The New Testament compared the apostles to the foundation stones of a building (a metaphor of the church), Christ being the chief Cornerstone. Ephesians 2:20, cf. Revelation 21:14.

The laying of foundation stones is done at the beginning of the construction and is not repeated. In this world, things like a crown of a king, property and some kinds of legal power can be inherited from the present possessor by someone of the next generation, or transferred from one person to another. To give a useful analogy, it is like the impossibility of transferring the musical genius of Beethoven or the poetical genius of Goethe to someone else.

Similarly, even if the primacy of the apostle Peter were admitted, his primacy would be unique to him and not transmitted to the next generation. Accordingly the Catholic dogma of the pope's primacy as Peter's successor is biblically unfounded. The uniqueness of the apostolate was specifically mentioned by Christ himself. Our Lord said, "I tell you the truth, at the renewal of all things, when the Son of Man sits on his throne in heavenly glory, you who have followed me will also sit on twelve thrones, judging the twelve tribes of Israel" (Matthew 19:28).

We should not lose sight of or forget the uniqueness of the apostolate which is emphasized in the New Testament. We can legitimately use the term "apostolic succession" only in the sense of pure and true preservation of the apostolic testimony and teaching.

Our considerations so far lead us to conclude that the above-mentioned threefold claims of the Roman Church regarding the papal primacy are unsubstantiated deduction from Matthew 16:18-19. There is one more point which makes the claims of the Roman Church look even more untenable.

In the gospel of Matthew there is a saying of Jesus which creates additional difficulty for the controversial Roman interpretation of Matthew 16:18-19. It is recorded in Matthew 18:18. Whereas in the first passage (16:18-19) Jesus appears to confer authority to Peter alone, in the second passage (18:18) he confers authority on all apostles without differentiation. Jesus seems to be saying the same thing in John 20:22-23 as well. In addition, Ephesians 2:20 and Revelation 21:10, 14 also clearly indicate that all twelve apostles are the foundation of the Church. According to these passages, all apostles, not just Peter alone, are the foundation on which the Church is built and all of them received the keys of heaven to "bind and loose."

As mentioned already, the intense struggle within the Church which has lasted for many centuries was the struggle of the successive bishops of Rome (popes) to claim and establish the papal supremacy over all other bishops, and to concentrate the absolute power in their own hands. They succeeded in the West completely by the 13th century. Subsequently the pope's struggle continued to expand the papal dominion over the Church throughout the world, but it achieved only a partial success. Yet the existence of the papal rule of the Roman Church around the world indicates that it has had a remarkable success indeed.

But is this a true kind of success? The popes also attempted and struggled hard to gain and keep the political power as well, but to their disappointment, failed to keep it. Rome's insatiable lust for power and tenacious claim to the supremacy reveal a pagan spirit. It is the spirit of the ancient Romans that conquered the world around the Mediterranean and built the Roman Empire. Only in such a pagan spiritual climate could such a papal claim to the supremacy be made and gratification found in the wielding of power and domination.

In contrast to that climate, the spirit of Jesus is revealed in his saying I quote it again. Our Lord told his disciples:

You know that the rulers of the Gentiles lord it over them, and their high officials exercise authority over them. It shall not be so among you. Instead, whoever wants to become great among you must be your servant, and whoever wants to be first among you must be your slave – just as the Son of Man did not come to be served, but to serve, and to give his life as a ransom for many.

<Matthew 20:24-28>
(See also Matthew 23:10-12.)

It is obvious that the Roman Church interpreted Matthew 16:18-19 and a few other favored biblical passages in terms of legal power and domination. This legal interpretation is incompatible with the spirit and teaching of Jesus.

We have seen that there are manifold difficulties with the monarchical papacy and the hierarchy of the Roman Church. We saw already that there is no historical evidence that the bishop of Rome exercised such a power in the earliest centuries. The monarchical papacy developed gradually in the course of history due to the historical and geographical situation and the will of the pope for power. We saw earlier that the popes used a series of audacious "forgeries" (forged historical documents) as a means to achieve their goal. If the primacy of the bishop of Rome was recognized since the earliest time as Rome asserts, we wonder why the use of multiple forgeries and the intense power struggles were needed. There has been no adequate explanation of this from Rome. Rome has only made claim after claim.

The pope and the hierarchical church (which is a clerical institution of different ranks from the pope downwards) claim to have the divinely invested absolute power, and enforce submission. The Roman Church claims that it is endowed with a threefold exclusive authority: first, the infallible teaching authority (the Church being the depository of saving truth); second, the authority to administer through sacraments the divine grace which is necessary for man's salvation; third, the authority to be the divinely authorized arbiter of man's fate after death, with the power to control through the mass and absolution man's period of stay in the pains of purgatory, and the power to enable him to go to heaven. The Roman Church claims to have the power to dispense saving merit from "the treasury of surplus merits" of the Virgin Mary, the saints and Christ which are at its disposal. Thus every Catholic has to depend on the Church for his or her knowledge of saving truths, for divine saving grace, and for the benefit of the treasury of merits. So the Roman Church is the arbiter of man's fate. What a difference between this aggrandized powerful Church and the church in the New Testament as the humble and lowly people of God and the modest "bride of Christ" who calls on the name of the Lord Jesus Christ!

This threefold claim of the Catholic Church should not be confused with the threefold claim of the pope, which we have discussed earlier. If a religious institution equipped with the powers just described is once established, it is in a position to dominate people with absolute power.

In the Roman Church the dogma of the papal primacy is not an isolated dogma, but is integrally linked to other major doctrines – the doctrines of the church, the apostolic succession, the sacred hierarchy, the magisterium, the infallibility of the church, the sacraments and the indulgence. The credibility of each of these doctrines and of the

Roman Catholic Church is at stake with the truth or otherwise of the dogma of the papal primacy. It is a puzzling phenomenon that this pagan institution with the name of the papacy still thrives and rules in the name of Christ approximately one half of the total number of the Christians in the world. In this troubled world many hard-to-explain things take place. Observed phenomena like this and our knowledge of the history of religions and the churches necessitate the reassessment of the organized institutional religions and the churches.

IX

THE CATHOLIC DOCTRINE OF THE SACRAMENT LACKS THE BIBLICAL BASIS

THE HISTORICAL FACTS AND EVENTS such as the Croatian Catholics' brutal atrocities committed to the non-Catholic Serb Christians and the despicable behaviours of the Catholic Church and Catholics with respect to the inhumane unjust institution of slavery and slave trade, serve as a disproof of the claimed efficacy of the sacrament of the Catholic Church in sanctifying its recipients (Catholics) and also throw discredit on the grandiose sacramental system of the Roman Catholic Church. I wish to present the biblical passages which, in my view, confirm our proposition.

I question the way the Roman Church legitimizes its ecclesiastical, sacramentalist religion by way of a particular interpretation of John 1:14 ("The Word became flesh.") and of Paul's concept of the church as the body of Christ, because the ecclesiastical, sacramentalist theme does not belong to the central theological thought of John and Paul.

Also the Roman interpretation of the Incarnation of the Word and of Paul's concept of the church is in my view biblically dubious. I ask the reader to note that I am not saying that the ecclesiastical, sacramentalist religion of the Roman Church is based on the Church's interpretation of John's and Paul's teachings in the New Testament. That is not the case. In the history of the Roman Catholic Church the ecclesiastical, sacramentalist system had developed first and only afterwards were its theological theories formulated to legitimize it. Obviously this procedure is an aberration, because the study of the Scripture and listening to what it says should come first, rather than "use" the Scripture afterwards to make up theological theories in order to legitimize what has been in existence for centuries. This is similar to the case of the monarchical papacy. The monarchical papacy had developed first; its theological theorizing came afterwards to legitimize it. This also is an aberration. We have discussed this question in chapters 1, 5 and 7.

Such being the case, the Roman Church's interpretation of the biblical passages which it asserts as referring to the church and the sacrament inevitably becomes manipulative because it reads its preconceived notions into the biblical passages. We call this a manipulative interpretation of the Scripture. If this is really what has happened, it means that a colossal evil has been committed by the Roman Catholic Church.

A fundamental question with regard to the sacrament is whether the sacrament is a sign and symbol of the invisible grace of God, or a channel (a means) of sanctifying the believers.

Of these three points, I think that the first and the second point have been made obvious to some degree through the narrative so far. In the following I am going to discuss the third point.

In comparison with other religions and other Christian churches, the Roman Catholic Church is clearly an ecclesiocentric and sacramentalist religion. The ritual sacramental system occupies the central and predominant place in the life of the Church and in the devotional life of faithful individual Catholics. There are seven sacraments in the Catholic Church: baptism, confirmation, eucharist, matrimony, penance, holy orders, and extreme unction.

The *Catechism of the Catholic Church* says, "The purpose of the sacraments is to sanctify men, to build up the body of Christ and, finally to give worship to God" (No. 1123). "Celebrated worthily in faith, the sacraments confer the grace that they signify. They are efficacious because in them Christ himself is at work" (No. 1127). By "efficacious" is meant that the sacraments work effectively, sanctifying the recipients and enabling them to love God and men and to be partakers in the holy divine nature, thus making them fit for blissful life in heaven. Even before going to heaven the sanctifying process has already started thanks to the objective *efficacy* of the sacraments of the Roman Church. It is also claimed, "Outside the Church there is no salvation" (Extra ecclesiam nulla salus). I make one more quotation from the *Catechism.* "The Church affirms that for believers the sacraments of the New Testament are necessary for salvation ... The fruit of the sacramental life is that the Spirit of adoption makes the faithful partakers in the divine nature ..." (No. 1129).

Through these quotations from the Catechism we see the important place the sacramental system holds in the Roman Church and in the lives of individual Catholics. We also see that the Catholic Church ascribes real effectiveness to the sacraments (especially to Baptism and the Eucharist, namely, the Mass) in sanctifying the recipients and making them Christ-like men and women. It is asserted that "the sacraments act *ex opera operato* ... It follows that the sacrament is not wrought by the righteousness of either the celebrant or the recipient, but by the power of God" (No. 1128).

Comment

In the nature of the case, it cannot be proved or known for certain whether or not the sacraments of the Catholic Church have real efficacy in making the recipients become morally better and Christ-like persons. We are keenly interested to see the evidence that the sacraments do indeed have such sanctifying effect. The assertions of the Catholic Church do not quite convince us of this efficacy. Not yet. Also we do not believe that the New Testament teaches plainly the sacramental efficacy in that sense. We would like to see the observable concrete fruits of love, changed life, sanctity and Christ-likeness. But we do not believe that we have seen more of such things in the predominantly Catholic communities and nations than in the non-Catholic regions. The Roman Church has canonized many men and women as saints, but we are not convinced that being canonized by the Catholic Church is the proof of their genuine sainthood.

We are inclined to think that the story of the Catholic Croatians' atrocities and savagery against the Orthodox Serb Christians and Jews amounts to a disproof of the efficacy of the Catholic sacraments and that it discredits the Catholic doctrine of the sacraments.

Here is another piece of what amounts to a disproof, in our view, of the efficacy of the sacraments of the Roman Church. It is the despicable behaviour of the Churches (both Roman and non-Roman) with respect to the cruel and unjust institution of slavery and the slave trade. It is a sobering historical fact that many millions of innocent Africans were kidnapped at gunpoint and sold as slaves. Cruelty, injustice and tragedy (from the Africans' point of view) involved in the practice of slave trade and slavery are beyond description.

The selling of Africans as salves against their will started in the 15th century with approval of the pope of Rome, Martin V and Nicholas V. A century later popes Paul III and Pius V forbade Catholic missionaries to have any part in the slave trade. Yet some Jesuit and Dominican priests continued the profitable trade. We have discussed this in chapter 3.

To make a long story short, neither the Catholic Church nor the Catholics, nor the non-Catholic churches, publicly condemned and openly opposed slavery and salve trade. In time there were a small number of individual Christians who realized the cruelty of slavery and the slave trade, and opposed them.

In the eighteenth century the movement against slavery was taken up seriously by the Quakers. The Quaker preacher John Woolman led a long campaign until his death in 1772. The Quakers' official title is "The Religious Society of Friends" and in some parts of the USA they are called "The Friends' Church". This religious sect originated in Britain and Ireland and spread to Europe and America. Lester Scherer, a historian of slavery, wrote a book on the history of slavery in America. I quote the first two passages from the book. "Only a few Christians, all of them Quakers, declared that slavery was incompatible with the Christian life for both salves and slave-owners." "By contrast, the most effective anti-slavery church was the Society of Friends ... Self-proclaimed and widely recognized as the nation's "conscience", the churches appeared to be saying that drinking whiskey or enjoying sex without marriage was more scandalous than holding people as slaves."

I draw attention to the fact that the Quakers have no ordained ministry, no set liturgy and creeds, and no sacraments as such. They do not believe in them. Therefore the Quakers do not have the benefit of sacraments. But they are devout Christians and have regular religious meetings. Although they are small in number, the Quakers have been widely known for their commitment to the promotion of peace and justice, and penal reform. In 1947 the Nobel Peace Prize was given jointly to the Friends Service Committee.

The shining example of love and Christian conscience of the Quakers as manifested in their movement against slavery (in contrast to the disappointing behaviour of the churches, Catholic and non-Catholic) lead us to a realistic appraisal of the institutional churches and their sacraments. We wonder, What is the use of the exalted sacraments of the Roman Church if "the sacramental grace" which is asserted to be efficacious *ex opera operato* do not produce the fruits of love in realistic terms among its recipients? We value the fruits of love and passion for social justice. We do not have much faith in abstract doctrinal theories of the institutional churches. We regard the contemptible behaviour of the institutional churches and their adherents with respect to slavery and the slave trade as a piece of disproof of the efficacy of their sacraments. It is extremely significant that the Quakers do not have the ordained ministry and the sacraments. How would the sacramentalists explain the love of fellow-man and the passion for justice of the Quakers, and the disappointing behaviour of the Roman Church and the Catholics?

Are not the passion for justice and acts of love what God consistently demanded through His prophets, namely, justice and mercy? Which side will be favoured by God in this respect, the Quakers or the institutional churches? God also said, "I desire mercy, not sacrifice" (Hosea 6:5). We have already seen this in the preceding chapters.

Jesus said, "Beware of the false prophets, who come to you in sheep's clothing, but inwardly are ravenous wolves. You will know them by their fruits" (Matthew 7:15-16). Also in his teaching about the Last Judgement, our Lord said, "I tell you the truth, whatever you did for one of the least of these brothers of mine, you did for me" (Matthew 25:40). But He (the Judge) will say to those on his left side, "Depart from me, you who are cursed, into the eternal fire prepared for the devil and his angels ... I tell you the truth, whatever you did not do for one of the least of these (brothers of mine) you did not do for me. Then they will go away to eternal punishment, but the righteous will go to eternal life" (Matthew 25:41, 45-46). The poor Africans who had been enslaved were among the least of the brothers of Jesus. We think that we have the authority of our Lord Jesus Christ that in the Last Judgement of God, both the righteous deeds and the sins of omission are the criteria of the Judgement.

In the New Testament we have a warning that the Judgement of God will begin with the church (I Peter 4:17). This is a warning to the authoritarian, self-aggrandizing church and its self-exalting hierarchy, and to other complacent churchmen.

In the foregoing chapters I have discussed in some detail and given a few reasons why I do not have much trust in some of the doctrines of the Roman Catholic Church. This is not unrelated to the issue we are considering in this chapter, but has some bearing on it, reinforcing my argument regarding the dubious efficacy of the sacraments of the Roman Church.

A shocking new report by a French news agency provides another piece of disproof. *Agence France-Presse* reported on March 23, 1977 that there were one million prostitutes in Italy and that in Rome alone there were 100,000 professional prostitutes. The Vatican and St. Peter's Basilica are located in Rome. Apparently the Holy See and a large number of holy places do not have spiritual and sanctifying effect as expected. The French news agency said that the numbers were given by an Italian women's organization for social morality. If this report is true, what does it seem to imply?

I give one more example of such disproof. The New York Times, on October 4, 1998, reported the result of a survey of the perceived degree of corruption of 85 countries conducted by an agency. I give a near duplication of the report written by the reporter, Barbara Crossette.

Transparency International, a small independent organization that has been tracking for four years how the public and international businesses view corruption worldwide, has published its largest survey to date, looking at 85 countries and ranking Denmark as the cleanest.

The 1998 Corruption Perception Index, like its predecessors, is a "survey of surveys," using a combination of studies of countries by how they are perceived.

The impressions this year are that of the top ten countries in the least corrupt category – Denmark, followed by Finland, Sweden, New Zealand, Iceland, Canada, Singapore, Netherlands, Norway and Switzerland – all but three are European. None of these ten least corrupt countries has traditionally been known as a Catholic country. All of them except Singapore and Switzerland have been known as Protestant countries. In Switzerland the Protestant and the Catholic populations are roughly the same in number.

At the other end of the scale, from the bottom up, are Cameroon, Paraguay, Honduras, Tanzania, Nigeria, Indonesia, Colombia, Venezuela, Ecuador, Russia, and Vietnam and Kenya in a tie.

Of these countries at the bottom Paraguay, Honduras, Colombia, Venezuela and Ecuador are in the predominantly Roman Catholic continent of Latin America.

The United States falls behind most European countries and Hong Kong, tying with Austria at 17th place. Transparency International is not alone in drawing attention to corruption through its branches in all parts of the world. In September, 1998 the United

Nations Development Program and the Organization for Economic Cooperation and Development joined hands to publish a study of anticorruption initiatives in 25 countries that serve as models in the battle against bribery, money laundering and other impediments to economic growth. But there is a new historical development today which makes things complicated, making our judgement difficult and even making our discussion so far look obsolete.

The New York Times published what it called an "Archive Article" on October 13, 2003 with the title, "Faith Fades Where It Once Burned Strong". It also gave an abstract of the 3,083 word article written by the reporter Frank Bruni. The abstract said in part, "The Changing Church Focuses on Christianity in Europe in the last quarter century. It finds withering of Christian faith in Europe and shift in its center of gravity to Southern Hemisphere; this is true in Roman Catholic Church as well as mainstream Protestant denominations ..."

We would like to see the sanctified life of more individual Catholics and a noticeably higher moral standard of the predominantly Catholic communities and nations than elsewhere. It we see that, we will reconsider our present low evaluation of the sacramental system of the Roman Catholic Church.

X

THE CATHOLIC CHURCH'S DOGMA OF TRADITION IS "A CONTEMPT OF THE WORD OF GOD"

THE IMMACULATE CONCEPTION AND THE Ascension of the Virgin Mary, the Transubstantiation of the elements of the Eucharist, Purgatory, the Primacy and the Infallibility of the Pope, and the dogma of Tradition – these are the dogmas which are unique to the Roman Catholic Church. These dogmas are not based on the plain teaching of the Holy Scripture.

At the fourth session (1546) of the Council of Trent (1545-63) which was convened by the pope Paul III in order to counter the Protestant Reformation and to deal with the issues deriving from it, the Council declared that the Council "receives and venerates with equal piety the books of the Old and the New Testament, and also the tradition concerning faith and morals as if dictated either orally by Christ or by the Holy Spirit and preserved by continual succession in the Catholic Church." Thus the unwritten "tradition" and the written books of the Holy Scripture were formally put on the same level of authority in respect to faith and morals. So the tradition was elevated to be an additional source of the divine revelation along with the Holy Scripture by the Roman Church. This indicates that the Catholic Church has realized that there are dogmas in the Church which are not taught in the Scripture. The Church of Rome felt the need of some means of legitimizing the unbiblical doctrines and ecclesiastical polity. The dogma of Tradition was devised to meet this need.

But that the Roman Church elevated "tradition" to be a new source of the divine revelation is a serious alteration of the traditional rule of the Church from the beginning. More seriously, this dogma of tradition contradicts the teaching of Christ who condemned the Pharisees for giving equal status to tradition alongside the Scripture. The situation is parallel. Christ condemned the Pharisees because they broke the command of God and nullified the word of God for the sake of their tradition (Matthew 15:6). Jesus said to the Pharisees, "Why do you break the command of God for the sake of your tradition?" (Matthew 15:3). The doctrines taught by tradition are "the commandments of men" (Matthew 15:9; Mark 7:6-7).

It is a surprise that the Roman Catholic Church ignored Christ's stern warning with respect to tradition. The Council of Trent put "tradition" on the same level with the Holy Scripture. But if it came to an issue between the Scripture and tradition, it was the Scripture that had to give way. Accordingly, in practice the Catholic Church places tradition even above the Scripture. If both are theoretically at the same level, the Scripture can no longer be the test for tradition.

In Colossians 2:8, the apostle Paul too warns against falling prey to what he called "philosophy of empty deceit" according to "the tradition of men". Likewise in Galatians 1:14, 16 Paul says that he abandoned his ancestral traditions when God reveled His Son in him. The apostle also says, "Do not go beyond what is written" (I Corinthians 4:6). "What is written" in this context probably refers to the apostolic testimony and teaching in writing. Peter placed Paul's writing alongside the Holy Scripture of the Old Testament (II Peter 3:15-16).

In the letter of Jude, the brother of James who probably was also a half brother of Jesus (Galatians 1:19), we read:

"Beloved, while I was making every effort to write you about our common salvation, I felt the necessity to write to you appealing that you contend earnestly for the faith which was once for all delivered to the saints."

<Verse 3>

Here Jude is urging the people of God to contend for and adhere to "the faith which was once for all delivered to the saints." Implied in this urging is that any addition to the faith which was one for all delivered to the saints or any change of the content of the faith is impermissible. "The faith which was once for all delivered to the saints" is based on the apostolic testimony, teaching and the Holy Scripture.

In the Church the apostolic testimony was a norm of doctrine. The apostolic testimony was not left to the recollections of the apostles alone. There was the guidance of the Holy Spirit; hence it was the testimony of the Holy Spirit as well. This theme is expounded in the great commissioning discourse (John 14-17) which Jesus gave at the Last Supper with his disciples. The apostles were to bear witness from their long acquaintance with Jesus, and the Holy Spirit also bears witness to him (John 15:26-27). Jesus promised them that the Holy Spirit would remind them of his words (John 16:13). Therefore the apostolic testimony and teaching are the norm of the doctrines of the Christian Church.

The apostolic doctrine of the Christian Church did not originate merely with the apostles' witness from their recollections but also with the guidance of the Holy Spirit. In the apostolic witnesses there were a common content and a principle which in hindsight we would call a theological principle. As it is so, even the chief apostle (Peter) could be withstood by a colleague when he betrayed the fundamental principle of the Gospel. (Galatians 2:11)

Above I said that the fact that the Roman Church elevated

"tradition" to the status of revealed truth along with the Holy Scripture is "a serious alteration of the traditional rule of the Church from the beginning". An elaboration of this statement is in order. The traditional rule of the Church from the beginning in this context concerns the doctrinal authority of the Church. To be more specific, it concerns whether the Church has authority to make a new doctrine (an article of faith) in addition to "the faith which was once for all delivered to the saints." The traditional understanding was that the Church has no such authority. I explain by giving examples. The apostolic age was followed by the age of the Church Fathers. It is necessary to examine what the Fathers taught with regard to this question.

St. Athanasius (296-373), the bishop of Alexandria, was a champion of the apostolic faith against Arianism and other heresies. Athanasius emphasized that "in the Holy Scriptures alone is the instruction of religion announced – to which let no man add, from which let no man detract—which are sufficient in themselves for the enunciation of the truth." To this statement the other Fathers would have given a cordial assent because the Fathers did not derive even one article of faith from the tradition outside the canon of the Holy Scripture. This has been historically attested. The Anglican bishop and theologian Charles Gore said, "I have never seen even one passage in any of the Fathers which contradicts this."

Another well-known Fathers, St. Basil (329-379) wrote, "it is a manifest falling from the faith, and a proof of arrogance, either to reject any of those things that Athanasius and St. Basil quoted above The teachings of the two Church Fathers were cited by Bishop Gore in his The Holy Spirit and the Church, 1924, p.173.) In our view this statement of Basil is applicable to the Roman Catholic Church that made a new dogma of Tradition in 1545 and has several more dogmas which have no biblical basis. In matters such as custom and discipline the Church could act freely as circumstance demands, but in the matter of the articles of faith the Church can do nothing except to preserve and teach "the faith which was once for all delivered to the saints."

The Council of Trent claimed that "the tradition concerning faith and morals ... (has been) preserved by continual succession in the Catholic Church." But this is merely a claim. We recall that the Gnostics, too, a major heretical sect in the early Christian centuries which posed a serious threat to the Church, claimed to have a special gnosis (knowledge) which derived from the apostles by a "secret tradition". The Church strongly denounced it. There is akinness between the two claims. The Roman Church has not been able to produce the concrete content of this tradition which has been allegedly preserved in the Catholic Church from the beginning and which is not in the written books of the Holy Scripture. Furthermore, if there were such tradition preserved in the Church from the beginning, it would more likely be in the Eastern (Orthodox) Church rather than the Western (Roman) Church because the East, not the West, was the main theatre of the activities of the apostles. But the Orthodox Church of the East does not make such a claim as the one made by the Roman Church in the West. I repeat that the Catholic Church has failed to present the concrete of the tradition allegedly preserved in that Church.

In time the Roman Church's definition of "tradition" changed. To trace the change of the definition of tradition in the Roman Church is beyond the scope of this book. Instead I quote two theologians regarding this question. The Anglican theologian Charles Gore again writes, "'tradition' means what at any period the Roman Church has come to hold, whatever the records of the past may be" (ibid. p. 208-9). The Catholic theologian August Bernhard Hasler also discussed this question in relation to the dogma of Infallibility of the Pope in particular. He writes, "'Tradition' to them (the defenders of the dogma) means no more than the prevailing opinions of the Church's magisterium. Perhaps they advanced this version of church tradition because that was what the dominant curial party wanted it. The curial party demands that the Bible be expounded along the lines acceptable to the teaching authority of the Church, that is, of the pope. In its constitution on faith the First Vatican Council explicitly sanctioned this ecclesiastical monopoly on interpretation" (How The Pope Became Infallible, 1979, by August Bernhard Hasler, p. 177).

Thus the definition of "tradition" changed in the Roman Church according to the need of the Church, especially of the pope. This reveals what kind of authority the pope wields in the Roman Catholic Church. It approaches despotism. Indications of papal despotism are not scarce. An example is the pope's decree that scholars must stop the historical investigation about the past of the papacy and the Church. On September 1, 1910 the pope Pius X issued the motu proprio (pope's letter) "Sacrorum antistitium", imposing on scholars an oath disavowing Modernism. Scholars were also compelled to make an oath by December 31 of the year to discontinue their historical investigation because their investigation was a peril to the doctrines of the Church. Most scholars took the oath under pressure, but there were about two dozen who hesitated to do so. They were subjected to the inquisition in Rome and there ensued a widespread harassment of them.

The redefinition of "tradition" according to the needs of the pope and the prohibition of historical research are just two examples which indicate the papal despotism. Why was the order to discontinue historical investigation necessary? The pope perceived that the historical investigation by scholars posed a threat to the papacy. The Catholic Church could not stand a historical scrutiny of scholars. Does this imply that Pius XX was aware that there was something about which to be embarrassed in the past of the papacy? So the past needed to remain hidden for the sake of the safety of the papacy. The fact that many items in the Vatican archives were destroyed arouses a similar suspicion. If there was nothing to hide, why was such a measure needed?

Earlier I quoted the church historian Adolf Harnack's statement regarding papal tyranny and ecclesiastical despotism. I quote again, "(The papacy) developed itself into the *autocratic* power in the Church ... ... and framed its legislation by means of numerous decretals. The pope afterwards, till the time of Innocent III, defended and strengthened their position in the Church amid severe but victorious struggles. No doubt, they had to hear many an anxious word from their most faithful sons; but the rise of the papacy to despotic power in the Church, and thereby to dominion over the world, was promoted by piety (of the faithful sons) and by all the ideal forces of the period" (History of Dogma (1900) by Adolf Harnack, Volume VI&VII, pp. 17-18).

There is another important related issue. God gave the Ten Commandments through Moses. The Second Commandment says, "You shall not make a carved image for yourself nor likeness of anything in the havens above, or on earth below, or in the waters under the earth. You shall not bow down to them or worship them" (Exodus 20:4; Deuteronomy 5:8). Yet, in most Catholic churches there are a number of images (representing Jesus, Mary, angels and saints). In St. Peter's Basilica of Rome, for example, one can see many images (statues). Is it right to place those statues in the church or anywhere if people are not told to bow down and venerate them? The Second Commandment clearly says, "You shall not make a carved image ... ..." Also, is it absolutely certain that no one adores any of these images in his or her mind? It appears that many Catholics frequently bend their knees before the statue of Mary, for example, and pray to it. These statues could be a snare to idolatry for the "weak" members of the Church. "Laying a snare" for the people of God was strictly forbidden by God in a variety of circumstances, for example Exodus 23:32-33, 34:12-13; Deuteronomy 7:25-26, 12:30; Joshua 23:11-13; Judges 2:2-3, 8:27.

The Roman Catholic Church is showing a contempt for the Word of God in allowing multiple images to be made and placed in the church, in putting the Holy Scripture and the tradition on the same level of authority, and in having a number of unbiblical dogmas of the Church. As far as its observable behaviours are concerned, the Roman Church has not demonstrated its respect for the word of God. Therefore what the prophet Isaiah said with regard to the ancient Israelites is relevant to the Church of Rome, "They rejected the law of the Lord of hosts, and despised the word of the Holy One of Israel" (5:24).

It can be said that in the Roman Catholic Church the pope and the Church have been made idols in that the papal church has exercised an authority not less than divine and claimed an allegiance such as men owe to God alone. The excessive self-aggrandizement and self-importance of the self-appointed "Vicar of Christ" and the Church approach "the idolatrous self-worship" spoken of by Reinhold Niebuhr.

Aware of the charge of idolatry, the Catholic Church attempts to justify its practice about images by invoking the Incarnation of the Son of God. The Catechism of the Catholic Church says, "By becoming incarnate, the Son of God introduced a new economy of images" (No. 2131). This is another example of that "inference" from the Incarnation whereby the Church of Rome tries to justify its new dogmas and practices which the Church in the apostolic times had not heard about. There is nothing in the New Testament which indicates or implies such an idea. Does the Incarnation of the Son of God justify adoring even the statues of Mary, other saints, and angels?

In hindsight we see that God provided the Holy Scripture as a safeguard against the tyranny of authority (such as the pope and the authoritarian church) in order to preserve the purity of the true religion and morality. The attempt to alter the Gospel of Christ started already in the days of the apostles. The apostle Paul gave a stern warning against such an attempt. Cf. Galatians 1:6-9. Also he said elsewhere, "Do not go beyond what is written" (1 Corinthians 4:6).

There is an exact parallel, in our view, between the provisions of the written laws of God through Moses and the provisions of the apostolic testimony and teaching in writing. Both are God's provisions. Commanded by God, Moses wrote down the laws of God and said to the Israelites of his days:

"Take this Book of the Law and place it beside the ark of the covenant of the Lord your God. There it will remain as a witness against you. For I know how rebellious and stiff-necked you are. If you have been rebellious against the Lord

*while I am still alive and with you, how much more will you
rebel after I die?"*

<Deuteronomy 31:26-27>

Moses also said:

*"Whatever I command you, you shall be careful to do; you
shall not add to nor take away from it."*

< Deuteronomy 12:32 cf. 4:2>

The situation in the days of the apostles and in the later days was similar. As we noted above, there were already attempts to change the Gospel of Christ while the apostles were still alive. The apostle John also wrote at the close of Revelation, warning neither to add nor to take away from the "the words of the prophecy of this book" (Revelation 22:18-19). The Gospel truth was already in danger of being altered and perverted. Therefore the written Scripture was an absolute necessity as a safeguard against human attempts to alter the true religion of God.

God provided this, namely, the Old and New Testament. With divine foresight and wisdom God commanded Moses and other prophets to write down for the posterity the word of God they received. For example, God said to the prophet Isaiah, "Go now, write it on a table for them, and inscribe it on a scroll, that for the days to come it may be an everlasting witness" (30:8). For another example:

*The word came to Jeremiah from the Lord, saying, "Thus says
the Lord, the God of Israel, Write all the words which I have
spoken to you in a book."*

<Jeremiah 30:1-2, cf. 36:1-4>

God who spoke to His people through the prophets and Christ have made His words thus spoken available to His people of later generations. So He has provided the Holy Scripture. If the revelation given is truly God's revelation, the Scripture as the record and testimony God gave to attest His revelation must be trustworthy. There is a remarkable passage in Isaiah which calls for our attention.

Seek and read from the book of the Lord:

Not one of these shall be missing;
None shall be without her mate.
For the mouth of the Lord has commanded,
And His Spirit has gathered them.

<34:16>

The Spirit of God has gathered the content of the Holy Scripture. If the mouth of the Lord has commanded and the Spirit of God has gathered the content of the Scripture, the status of the Holy Scripture is unique. Then what would the status of "tradition" be, which has allegedly been in the Catholic Church? How is the Catholic dogma of "tradition" to be assessed, according to which the tradition and the Holy Scripture are equal as the source of the Divine revelation? This Catholic dogma which was designed as an afterthought to legitimize those doctrines and practices in the Roman Church which are not found in the Scripture, is contempt of the Word of God.

In the Middle Ages the Catholic Church tried to keep the Holy Scripture away from the lay people. In a meeting in Toulouse (France) in 1229 the Roman Church formally forbade the lay people to possess or read the Scripture. For a layman to possess or read the Scripture was an offence punishable severely. During the five-century long Inquisition the offender was tried and put to death by burning. Until a few decades ago, the general tendency in the Roman Church was to discourage the reading of the Bible by laity. The picture today is not clear, varying to a degree from country to country.

In our view this is contrary to the will of Jesus our Lord. In the Synoptic gospels we count at least 14 passages in which our Lord approvingly refers to the reading of Scripture. We cite a few:

"Have you not read this Scripture?"

<Mark 12:10>

"Is this not the reason you are mistaken, that you do not understand the Scripture?"

<Mark 12:24>

"Have you not read in the book Moses how God spoken to him ...?"

<Mark 12:26>

"Have you not read that He Who created them from the beginning made them male and female ..."

<Matthew 19:4>

"What is written in the Law? How do you read it?"

<Luke 10:26>

Jesus sometimes called the Scripture "the law and the prophets" or "Moses and the prophets" (Luke 24:27, 16:29, 31).

How are we to interpret these sayings of Jesus? Our interpretation is that these sayings imply that:

1. Our Lord took it for granted that every person had a right to read the Scripture.
2. Our Lord assumed that his hearers had or should have had some knowledge about the content of the Scripture.
3. It is not right that people's access to the Scripture is barred by any authoritarian body.

We find in the Scripture that it is God Himself who has provided the Holy Scripture, and that God's purpose in providing the Scripture is that His People read or hear the words of God and obtain true knowledge about God and His ways. Cf. Deuteronomy 31:9-13. Those ancient Israelites at the time of Moses who were not able to read and for whom the words of God in writing was not available, were to hear others read the words of God for them.

How are we to view the decision of the Catholic Church that strictly forbade the people to read or possess the Holy Scripture? In our view such behavior of the church hierarchy is despotic, and amounts to disobedience to and an insult of God's command who gave these and other prescriptions about the Scripture. Is the pope really the Vicar of Christ and the Infallible teacher of the Christian Church as he claims? We must say a firm "No.

XI

THE APOSTOLIC SUCCESSION AND THE THREEFOLD MINISTRY OF THE ROMAN CATHOLIC CHURCH

THE TERM "APOSTOLIC SUCCESSION" REFERS to the proposition that the ministry of the Christian Church is derived from the apostles by a continuous succession of bishops. The Roman Catholic Church holds the doctrine of apostolic succession and claims that this succession has been maintained by a continuous series of bishops from the beginning. The Orthodox Church and part of the Anglican Church also hold this doctrine. Bishops of these Churches are fond of calling themselves "successors of the apostles." Bishops of the Catholic Church are so-called "monarchical bishops". In the Catholic Church the doctrines of apostolic succession and of monarchical bishops are inseparably tied. The Catechism of the Catholic Church says, "Just as the office which the Lord confided to Peter alone, as first of the apostles, destined to be transmitted to his successors, is a permanent one, so also endures the office, which the apostles received, of shepherding the Church, a charge destined to be exercised without interruption by the sacred order of bishops" (No.862).

But these dual claims made by the Roman Catholic Church are not supported by the biblical evidence. Here we limit our attention to the claim that the bishops have by divine institution taken the place of the apostles. (The claim of the papal primacy will be dealt with separately in Appendix D.)

Most scholars who have studied this issue are of the opinion that the claim of the Roman Church cannot be substantiated by the Scripture. The term "apostolic succession" is not found in the New Testament and there is no clear indication of the idea in the New Testament. Acts 20:17, 28 and Titus 1:5-7 reveal that the office of elder (presbyter) and the office of bishop (episcopes, overseer) are interchangeable, which means that in the days of the apostles the elder and the bishop were identical. They were mature Christian men who were appointed to supervise the local church (I Peter 5:1-4). Then, gradually one elder, probably the teaching member of the group, assumed presidency to become the "bishop" with special powers and honour. This is a later development. During the lifetime of the apostles, this did not take place. In the New Testament, the bishop is not a different office from the elder. There are more passages which throw light on this question. Cf. Philippians 1:1; I Timothy 3:1-4, 8-13. Therefore we can say safely that in the New Testament the episcopate (the office of bishop) is not a distinct, higher officer above the presbyter (the elder).

There is a near consensus among non-Catholic theologians that the Catholic doctrines of the apostolic succession and the monarchical bishop have no biblical, nor church historical basis. Even some open-minded Catholic theologians admit this. For example Hans Kueng writes, "A careful investigation of the New Testament sources in the past hundred years has shown that this church constitution, centered on the bishops, is by no means directly willed by God or given by Christ, but is the result of a long and problematical historical development. It is human work and therefore in principle can by changed" (Hans Kueng: *The Catholic Church*, 2001, p.19).

Another Catholic theologian Piet Fransen expressed a similar view. He has made a historical study of the development of various ministries in the apostolic and post-apostolic Church. His is a rather comprehensive and basic study and therefore is worth quoting. "The Churches founded by Paul and others, like the Church of Rome, gradually came to have a governing body, called elders (presbyteroi) and later bishops (episkopoi), as in Acts ... These Churches developed more slowly towards the monarchical structure adopted in Asia Minor. This delay seems to be attested by Clement of Rome and in *Hermas*, and still later in the customs of the Churches of Alexandria and perhaps Lyons, where the installation and ordination of the bishop was the work of the elders. These customs may have lasted till the 3rd century. This evidence does not permit us to affirm that the hierarchy of orders, e.g. monarchical bishop, college of elders and deacons, was a divine institution in the strict sense, or even an institution of the apostolic Church, considered as a norm of later Churches."

Fransen's account is valuable because it is based on biblical and historical evidence. The fact that his presentation is contained in the Encyclopedia of Theology edited by Karl Rahner (1975) is significant since Rahner is a highly respected theologian in the Roman Church. (p. 1128)

If what I have presented above is true, then not only the doctrine of the apostolic succession of the Roman Church but also the doctrine of the threefold ministry of bishop, priest (elder) and deacon is to be questioned, and even the Roman Church's dogma of the papal primacy is not beyond dispute. The Catholic Church's claims about these hotly disputed issues are made in, for example, No. 880 and 881 of *the Catechism*. "When Christ instituted the Twelve, he constituted (them) in the form of a college or permanent assembly, at the head of which he placed Peter, chosen from among them. Just as by the Lord's institution, St. Peter and the rest of the apostles constitute a single apostolic college, so in the like fashion, the successors of the apostles, are related with and united to one another ... This pastoral office of Peter and other apostles belongs to the Church's very foundation and is continued by the bishops under the primacy of the Pope."

In our view, the evidence in the New Testament is not supportive of the Catholic claim. As we are not able to discuss all aspects of this controversial issue here, we will limit our consideration and focus on the main point. According to the New Testament, the apostolate is a unique office and as such cannot be shared with others or passed on to the later generations. Regarding the uniqueness of the apostles I quote an explanatory account in the Ryrie Study Bible (p.1460), "The word 'apostle' means 'one sent forth', and ambassador who bears a message and who represents the One who sent him. The qualification included:

1. Seeing the Lord and being an eye-witness to His resurrection (Acts 1:22; I Corinthians 9:1);

2. Being invested with miraculous sign-gifts (Acts 5:15-16, 14:3, 19:11-12; Romans 15:18; II Corinthians 12:12; Hebrews 2:3-4). Of these passages, I quote only one here: 'The things that mark an apostle – signs, wonders and miracles – were done among you with great perseverance' (II Corinthians 12:12);

3. Being chosen by the Lord or the Holy Spirit (Matthew 10:1-2; Acts 1:25-26)."

Healing and other miraculous gifts, such as prophecy and exorcism, are abundantly attested in the apostolic church, related, like the apostolic witness, to the special dispensation of the Holy Spirit. But they are missing in the post-apostolic church. Do the pope and the bishops of the Catholic Church perform miracles? Also the apostle's authority depended on the fact that he had been commissioned by Christ either in the days of his flesh (Matthew 10:5, 29:19) or after he had risen from the dead (Acts 1:24, 9:15).

The apostle Paul says, "The Church is built on the foundation of the apostles and prophets" (Ephesians 2:20). The apostle Paul is using a metaphor of building here and likens the Church to a house or a building. As everyone knows, foundation stones are laid on the ground at the beginning of the construction of a building or a house. Laying of a foundation is not repeated; therefore no more foundation stones are needed for the building. The foundation stones will sit and remain there and cannot be succeeded to or inherited by others in later generations. Ministers of the Church, no matter how distinguished they may be, cannot be foundation stones of the spiritual building called the Church. They are bricks, lumber or tiles of the building, so to speak. The foundation stones are to be clearly distinguished from the bricks, lumbers and tiles. According to Revelation, the last book of the New Testament, the names of the apostles are engraved on the twelve foundation stones of the Holy City, Jerusalem, coming down out of heaven from God (Revelation 21:14). Our Lord said that the apostles will sit on twelve thrones when He sits on His glorious throne at the Last Judgment (Matthew 19:28).

Thus the apostolate is a unique position and office. No minister of the Church can rightly claim to be a successor of the apostle. The Church of Rome has formulated its doctrines of the episcopacy and the papacy based on false claims including this one. The doctrine of apostolic succession is to be rejected as biblically unfounded.

Based on chapter 12 of I Corinthians, Romans 12:6-8 and Ephesians 4:11-12, theologians have presented what they perceived to be the apostle Paul's concept of the Church and the ministry of the Church. The Pauline churches were largely communities with free charismatic ministries. According to Paul "every" Christian was endowed with his appropriate gift of the Spirit for his own ministry (I Corinthians 12:7 and 11). So in the Pauline churches there were various forms of ministry: for preaching, teaching, giving help, administering pastoral care and so on. These were all necessary "for the equipment of the saints for the work of service (ministry)" (Ephesians 4:12).

But after the apostolic times, there gradually emerged a class of clergy who were increasingly separated from the people; the lay people came to be dominated by the clergy who monopolized ecclesiastical offices and tasks. This represents a deformation of the ministry in the New Testament sense of the word. The development of Eucharistic worship provides a good illustration of this deformation.

According to Paul's first epistle to the Corinthians, the Eucharist (the Lord's Supper) was initially part of corporate worship in which everyone had a role to play and each was as important as the other. But soon after the departure of the apostles the Eucharist became something celebrated by the priest (presbyter, episcopes) alone in the presence of the passive people who were looking on. Thus a radical change in the concept of the ministry and of the celebration of the eucharist took place. Gradually the Roman Church as a sacerdotal, ritualistic (sacramentalist) church dominated by the clergy emerged and was established.

According to the Catholic doctrine, the order of clergy is essential for the Church. But the New Testament conceives of the Church as the people of God; hence the clergy is not an essential part of it. This can be seen in, for example, Acts 14:23 and 20:28. As we have already discussed the latter passage, we limit our attention to Acts 14:23. Paul and Barnabas "appointed elders in every church" of South Galatia. Implied in the passage is that the churches were there before elders were appointed in them. Clergy are not essential to the Church in the sense that the Church cannot exist without them. Of course, some ministry is necessary in the sense that the Church cannot be fully effective for its tasks without it. In Rome, too, at the time when the apostle Paul wrote his epistle to the Christian community in Rome, there was apparently no order of clergy (bishop or elder) yet. We turn to consider the next related question, How and when did the so-called monarchical episcopacy as we see it in the Roman Church emerge? There is some mystery about the origin of the episcopacy. We saw earlier that in the days of the apostles the episcopos (the overseer, the bishop) of the church was not a distinct higher officer above the presbyter (elder). The two terms were interchangeable.

But early in the post apostolic period the threefold ministry of bishop – presbyter – deacon emerged. What is certain is that this threefold ministry appeared "after" the departure of the apostles. I quoted above the two Catholic theologians Hans Kueng and Piet Fransen who presented the view that the episcopacy in the sense of the monarchical bishop has no biblical basis and is not a divine institution. I quote Kueng again, "it cannot be verified that the bishops are successors of the apostle in the direct and exclusive sense. It is historically impossible to find in the initial phase of Christianity and unbroken chain of laying on of hands from the apostles to the present-day bishops. Historically, rather, it can be demonstrated that in a first postapostolic phase, local presbyter-bishops became established alongside prophets, teachers, and other ministers as the sole leaders of the Christian communities; thus a division between "clergy" and "laity" took place at an early stage. In a further phase the monarchical episcopate, of an individual bishop, increasingly displaced a plurality of presbyter-bishops in a city and later throughout the region of a church ... The Eucharist could no longer be celebrated without a bishop. The division between clergy and people was now a fact" (ibid. p. 21-22).

So for St. Ignatius (the bishop of Antioch in the early 2nd century), bishop, presbyter and deacon were already distinct. The threefold ministry also emerged in some churches of Asia Minor. By the middle of the 2nd century it appears that the monarchical episcopacy was adopted in major centres of Christianity in Asia Minor. Probably Ignatius was the first monarchical bishop in Syria and he is the earliest witness to the threefold ministry. The bishop became the supervising leader of a number of local churches in a region (later a diocese), not just of one local church. The leader of a local church was the elder (presbyter).

A crucial point to note is that Ignatius did not say that the episcopacy is a divine institution, and he does not mention the apostolic succession. Instead he emphasized the bishop's unifying authority in perilous times when the Church faced a crisis due to the heresies of Donatism, Gnosticism and Judaistic teaching which were rapidly spreading. He seemed to be saying that the monarchical episcopacy was the best way for the Church to weather the difficult times.

Through historical research it has been confirmed that the apostolic succession as a theory of ministry in the Church was absent in the 1st century and in much of the 2nd century. It arose during the last quarter of the 2nd century. All succession lists were complied late in the 2ne century. Clement of Rome (a contemporary of St. Ignatius of the East) appeals to a simple form of apostolic succession, but his letters betray no knowledge of the monarchical episcopacy and the threefold ministry of the church. In his famous letter to the Corinthians Clement makes it clear that for him, that is, in Rome and in Corinth, the titles "bishops" and "presbyters" refer to the same persons. Clemet's letter is regarded as extremely valuable in tracing the development of "early Catholicism" in the West. There was some difference in the development between the East and the West.

The apostolic succession in the sense meant by the Roman Church nowadays appears to be first found in the West in the 3rd century. We have a "testimony" of Jerome, a famous biblical scholar and translator, from the 4th century, "The presbyter is the same as the bishop, and before parties had arisen in religion, the churches were governed by the Senate of the presbyters." (Anderson Scott: Romanism and the Gospel, 1937, p. 149)

As I mentioned above, long before the time of Jerome the movement had begun which led to the setting of one bishop above his copresbyters. The movement started in the East and spread to the West.

The apostolic Succession as claimed by the Roman Church regulates not only the ecclesiastical government and the teaching authority of the Church, but also the liturgy namely, the sacramental system of the Church; and virtually the entire religion of the Catholic Church. Therefore if the doctrine of the Apostolic Succession turns out to be biblically and historically unfounded, it means that the grand edifice of the Roman Catholic Church is actually made of clay.

In any case, the New Testament is not concerned to indicate the method of transmission or succession of the ministry of the Church. Does this mean that things like the shape of the ministry and the constitution of the Church are secondary matters and they can be devised by the Church to meet its needs under varying circumstances? The main concern of the New Testament is to ensure that the apostolic faith, which is possible only through preserving and adhering to the apostolic testimony and teaching be deposited in its writing. The distinguished New Testament scholar F.F. Bruce rejects the Catholic doctrines of the apostolic succession and the apostolic church as biblically groundless and false, and says, "The true apostolic succession is the steadfast continuing in the apostles' teaching and fellowship. An apostolic church is one in which the apostolic teaching is maintained ... Provision is made in the New Testament for the maintenance of a true apostolic succession in this sense; see, for example, II Timothy 2:2, where Paul instructs Timothy to impart the teaching which he had received from Paul to faithful men, who shall be able to teach others also. So the continuity of apostolic teaching would be maintained from generation to generation, the canonical Scripture providing a permanent standard by which the apostolicity of this transmitted teaching would be tested. It was to safeguard the pure transmission of the apostolic teaching that emphasis was first laid on the importance of the continuous succession of bishops in a church, especially in a church of apostolic foundation" (F.F Bruce: Answers to Questions (1972), p. 154).

Our inevitable conclusion is that the apostolic succession of persons, the monarchical episcopacy, and the threefold ministry of the Catholic Church are man-made institutions.

We saw above how the division between "clergy" and "laity" (people) took place early in the postapostolic Church. After the ecclesiastical law of clerical celibacy was enforced early in the Middle Ages, the separation of the clergy from the people became more rigid and the priestly caste was firmly established. But according to the New Testament, the apostle Peter and other apostles took their wives along with them in their evangelistic journeys (I Corinthians 9:5).

As the ordained clergymen alone were authorized to celebrate the eucharist and other sacraments which were held to be the channels of the divine grace essential for salvation, the lay people were made powerless in the Church and dependent on and subordinate to the clergy. The Roman Church became a clerical church with a hierarchical, monarchical organization which culmincated in the autocratic papacy. The church as "the people of God", as taught in the New Testament, was ignored and pushed aside. Thus and imperious, authoritarian church emerged which may be regarded as the ecclesiastical version of the ancient Roman Empire as far as the structure of ecclesiastical government, jurisprudence and authoritarianism are concerned.

XII

THE PERSONALIST RELIGION AGAINST THE ECCLESIASTICAL SACRAMENTALIST RELIGION

(A Debate with the Catholic Church)

1

I PRESENT THE PROPOSITION THAT CHRISTIANITY is a personalist religion. This proposition is grounded on the two fundamental biblical affirmations. The first is that God is attested in the Bible as a living personal God of moral character. The second is that the New Testament and especially the Gospel attested in the four gospels clearly conceive our relationship with God in personal terms.

The assertion that the God in the Bible is a personal God is grounded on the fundamental biblical affirmations as follows:

1. God spoke through the prophets and communicated His will to the people of Israel, chosen by God for a special purpose.

Prior to that, God called individual persons (Abraham, Isaac, Jacob, Moses, David and others) and made promises to them. God called Abrahams "My friend" (Isaiah 41:8). Only a personal God can do such things. The God of the Bible speaks.

2. God intervened in the human history with mighty acts, delivering the Israelites from the bondage in Egypt and entering into a covenant relationship with them. God also intervened repeatedly after that.

3. God revealed Himself to be "the compassionate and gracious God, slow to anger, abounding in love and faithfulness" (Exodus 34:6). Only a personal God can be such a God. Compassion, grace, love and faithfulness are the characteristic qualities which only which only a personal being has. A self-conscious being who has such qualities, whether divine or human, is to be conceived as a person. According to the Scripture, God revealed Himself to be such a God. Only a personal God can reveal something about Himself to others.

4. The fact that God has a Name and revealed it to Moses indicates that God is a Person. (Exodus 3:13-15, 6:3) The revealed Name of God is Yahweh (Exodus 3:15).

5. God introduced Himself to Israel (and to all nations of the earth), urging them to be saved: "And there is no other God besides Me, and a Saviour; there is none except Me. Turn to Me, and be saved, all the ends of the earth; I am God, and there is no other" (Isa 45:21-22). Only a personal God can introduce Himself to others and save.

6. God was in Jesus Christ, a living person, definitively revealing Himself as a loving, gracious, personal God, forgiving sins and saving men. "God so loved the world that He gave His only begotten Son" (John 3:16). Only a personal God can love like this.

7. The biblical teaching that the church (the people of God) is "the bride of Christ" reveals that Christianity is a personalist religion before being anything else. What is more personal

than the relationship between the bride and the bridegroom? Love is the most personal affair.

8. According to the biblical testimony God revealed Himself as a moral God, demanding justice and mercy from man and his society. Morality is applicable only in interpersonal relationship and in the world of persons. A moral God must be a personal God.

9. It is admitted as true that God is a transcendent, incomprehensible mystery. But on the basis of God's self-revelation in these multi-phases we are justified to characterize God as a Person and to call His relationship to man a personal one. Although there was a development in the biblical concept of God, a basic substratum in the concept of God remains essentially constant, namely, that God is a personal God, and God is increasingly conceived of in personal categories like mercy, grace and love.

In the Old Testament God made His covenant with Israel, His people, and not with individual Israelites. But God dealt with His people as His son or daughter. Thus there was a personalization. In Jeremiah 3:20 we read, "Is not Ephraim My dear son, the child in whom I delight? ... My heart yearns for him; I have great compassion for him," declares the Lord. Hosea 11:8 reads, "How can I give you up, O Ephraim? How can I surrender you, O Israel? ... My heart is turned over within me; all My compassions are kindled."

10. The God who is being testified in the Holy Scripture is a God who weeps. Read Isaiah 16:6-14 and Jeremiah 48:29-44, 8:21-9:11. God weeps and laments over the destruction (judgement) He has had to bring on sinful people. God in the biblical testimony is not an "impassible" God who is incapable of feeling, emotion and pain. When His people and even the heathens like Moabites suffer, God suffers too. "When my people are crushed I am crushed, too. I mourn and horror grips Me" (Jeremiah 8:21). Therefore it is not utterly a surprise that this God initiated the redemption project for the

fallen mankind through Christ. "God demonstrates His own love toward us, in that while we were yet sinners, Christ died for us" (Romans 5:8). The redemption of mankind through Christ is God's own undertaking.

11. In the New Testament there is a personalization in another sense. Christ died for the salvation of mankind. But Christ's salvation is individually appropriated. "For God so loved the world, that He gave His only begotten Son, that whoever believes in Him should not perish, but have eternal life" (John 3:16). The apostle Paul went further and said, "I have been crucified with Christ; and it is no longer I who live, but Christ lives in me; and the life which I now live in the flesh I live by faith in the Son of God, who loved me and gave Himself for me" (Galatians 2:20). In our present context of consideration the main point is, "Christ lives in me; (He) loved me and gave Himself for me." This is a personalization of the salvation through Christ's death. The same is true of God's love. God's love is personalized. It is not just that God loves mankind or God loves us. I should say, "God loves me and I love God". So there is a personal relation between God and me. it is similar to the relation between a father and a son. This is the gospel truth taught by Christ himself. Christianity is a personalist religion.

12. Christ claimed to be the good shepherd. "I am the good shepherd. The good shepherd lays down his life for the sheep … I know my sheep and my sheep know me" (John 10:11, 14). Christ also said, "The shepherd of the sheep … calls his own sheep by name" (John 10:3). The meaning of this allegory is clear and does not need an explanation. The good shepherd calls his own sheep by name, for each one is not just one of many in the flock. Likewise Christ knows each and every believer by name. He knows your name and mine. An individual believer is not just one among many to Christ; he or she is individually known to Christ and individually precious. Thus Christ's relationship to an individual believer is a personal one. Christianity is a personalist religion.

The Parable of the Lost Sheep which was told by Christ illustrates further this truth (Matthew 18:12-14; Luke 15:3-10). The shepherd who had a hundred sheep left the ninety-nine in the open country and went out to find the one lost sheep.

Conclusion

Based on these biblical testimonies we are entitled to conclude that God is a Person and Christianity is a personalist religion. The personalist religion of the Holy Scripture and "the sacramentalist religion" of the Roman Catholic Church represent two distinct lines of thought; and it seems to me that it is difficult to reconcile the two fully.

The Catholic Church too concedes that God is a personal God. But its metaphysical thought qualifies its concept of a personal God. It is not a personal God in the strict sense of the word. This is apparent in the fact that the most distinctive characteristic of Roman Catholicism is that it is "an ecclesiastical sacramentalist religion" which tends to impersonalize the religion, and that the Catholic Church gave the official sanction to the philosophy of Thomas Aquinas who accepted the ontological metaphysics of the Greek philosopher Aristotle and identified God with "Being". Aristotle's ontology (the science of being) is an abstract impersonal system of thought.

After having said the above, I hasten to add that it goes without saying that the personality of God and that of humans are not to be conceived as completely similar in all respects. God is the Creator and the human beings are His creatures. Undoubtedly there are some aspects in God' personality which are beyond the human comprehension. Man as a finite creature comprehends God only within limits. God has revealed Himself to humans only to the extent that they can comprehend and it is necessary for the purpose of Divine-human encounter and relationship. All metaphysical theories of philosophers about God are human speculations and their verity is not beyond dispute.

2

I question the way the Roman Church legitimizes its ecclesiastical, sacramentalist religion by way of a particular interpretation of John 1:14 ("The Word became flesh.") and of Paul's concept of the church as the body of Christ, because the ecclesiastical, sacramentalist theme does not belong to the central theological thought of John and Paul. Also the Roman interpretation of the Incarnation of the Word and of Paul's concept of the church is in my view biblically dubious. I ask the reader to note that I am not saying that the ecclesiastical, sacramentalist religion of the Roman Church is based on the Church's interpretation of John's and Paul's teachings in the New Testament. That is not the case. In the history of the Roman Catholic Church the ecclesiastical, sacramentalist system had developed first and only afterwards were its theological theories formulated to legitimize it. Obviously this procedure is an aberration, because the study of the Scripture and listening to what it says should come first, rather than "use" the Scripture afterwards to make up theological theories in order to legitimize what has been in existence for centuries. This is similar to the case of the monarchical papacy. The monarchical papacy had developed first; its theological theorizing came afterwards to legitimize it. This also is an aberration.

Such being the case, the Roman Church's interpretation of the biblical passages which it regards as referring to the church and the sacrament inevitably becomes manipulative because it reads its preconceived notions into the biblical passages. I call this a "manipulative" interpretation of the Scripture. If this is really what has happened, it means that a colossal evil has been committed by the Roman Catholic Church.

I will deal with this question along with others. To begin with, let us consider the Catholic concept of the sacraments and the so-called "sacramental grace."

A fundamental question with regard to the sacraments is whether a sacrament is a sign and symbol of the invisible grace of God, or a channel (a means) of transmitting the saving benefits such as the forgiveness of sins, the gift of the Holy Spirit and the new birth (sanctification).

The latter interpretation is called "sacramentalism" and the Roman Church advocates this interpretation. But it is difficult to give a definitive answer to this question one way or the other because the New Testament passages which refer to the sacraments (baptism and the Lord's Supper) use varied expressions, including symbolical ones, and they are open to different interpretations. If it were not so, there would not have arisen heated disputes in the church history over the sacraments among the different denominations.

So let us examine the various features in the New Testament references to the sacraments. We will examine the case of baptism first. Involved in the question of baptism are the meaning of baptism, and the assumed benefits of baptism such as the forgiveness of sins, receiving the gift of the Holy Spirit and the new birth of the recipient of baptism.

We begin with the question of the baptismal formula. According to the Acts of the Apostles and the epistles of Paul, the apostles baptized the new believers in the name of the Lord Jesus or Jesus Christ (Acts 8:16, 19:5, 10:48; 1Corinthians 6:11). But according to Matthew's gospel, Jesus commanded the apostles to baptize by the Trinitarian formula, namely, in the Name of the Father, of the Son and of the Holy Spirit (28:19). How are we to explain this discrepancy? And which of the two formulas is to be used by the church? In the post-apostolic period, the Christian churches adopted the Trinitarian formula. But we should not forget that the apostles of Christ themselves baptized the new believers in the name of the Lord Jesus Christ.

Next, let us consider the meaning of Baptism. The commonly accepted meaning of Baptism is that Baptism is a rite of initiation which marks the entry of a new believer into the church. For a person to receive Baptism is an expression of his repentance and faith and also an act of commitment to the discipleship of Christ. But beyond that the picture is not so clear. There are references to Baptism in all four gospels and in the epistles, but the meaning of Baptism is expressed in diverse ways.

A crucial question regarding the sacrament of baptism is, are there real benefits which are imparted to the recipient of baptism? If there are, what are they? To this question, the Catholic Churches and the non-Catholic Churches give different, almost opposite answers. The Catholic Churches including the Greek Orthodox Church and parts of the Anglican Church assert that the sacrament of baptism imparts the sacramental grace (i.e. benefits) to the recipient of baptism. The main benefits of baptism which the Catholic Churches ascribe to baptism are the forgiveness of sins, the gift of the Holy Spirit and the new birth, namely, a change in moral and spiritual character. The Roman Catholic Church even asserts that "the sacraments act *ex opera operato* (literally: by the very fact of the action's being performed" (*The Catechism*, No. 1128). The sacraments are held to "make present efficaciously the grace that they signify" (No. 1084). The phrase *ex opera operato* indicates that the sacraments are efficacious objectively and almost automatically when they are celebrated by the priest of the church. The non-Catholic Churches reject this concept of sacrament as magical and pagan. They conceive the sacrament of baptism by and large as a sign and symbol of the invisible grace of God, besides being a rite of entry into the church. The Roman Church legitimizes its doctrine of the sacrament by referring to its "infallible teaching authority" allegedly bestowed upon it by Christ.

It is difficult to make a definitive statement about the sacrament because the picture in the New Testament is not quite clear. Each of the disputing Churches claims the biblical support. For instance, with regard to the relation of baptism to the forgiveness of sins and receiving the gift of the Holy Spirit, we read in Acts 2:38, "And Peter said to them, 'Repent, and let each of you be baptized in the name of Jesus Christ for the forgiveness of your sins; and you shall receive the gift of the Holy Spirit". This passage seems to be saying that by being baptized in the name of Jesus Christ a new believer is forgiven his sins and receives the gift of the Holy Spirit. However, elsewhere in the New Testament we find different teachings. Acts 10:43-48 and Galatians 3:1-3 indicate that an individual person receives the Holy Spirit by hearing and believing the word of the (apostolic) preaching.

Acts 19:4-6 indicates that a believer receives the Holy Spirit by the laying on of hands of the apostles after baptism. Acts 3:19, 5:31 and Luke 24:47 say that one receives the forgiveness of sin by repentance. In Luke 11:13 Jesus said that one receives the Holy Spirit by asking the Heavenly Father for the Holy Spirit.

In John 7:38, Jesus said that whoever believes in him will receive the Holy Spirit. Regarding the new birth (regeneration) of the believer, I Peter 1:23 and James 1:18 say that the new birth is effected by the word of God, and John 3:5 and Titus 3:5 say that it is through water and the Holy Spirit. The Roman Church usually takes a reference to "water" or "washing" as a reference to baptism. But this interpretation is not to be taken as referring to baptism by water. Titus 3:5 reads, "He (God) saved us, not on the basis of deeds which we have done in righteousness, but according to His mercy, by the washing of regeneration and renewing by the Holy Spirit. In the present context of our inquiry the question is whether "washing" in this verse should be taken as a reference to baptism, and whether it says that the believer's regeneration (new birth) is achieved by baptism. As sin is a spiritual matter man's sin is not of the nature that it can be washed away by water or burned out by fire, and our new birth is not achieved by the mere rite of baptism but by the Holy Spirit of God who is at work in it. The main role in baptism is played by the Holy Spirit rather than water. In the Christian baptism a natural thing like water participates as a sacramental element and becomes a bearer of spiritual meaning and power. Its power is symbolical. This argument is presented from the perspective that conceives the sacrament as a sign and symbol of the invisible grace of God. Regarding the relation between regeneration and sanctification, we understand that regeneration represents the beginning stage of the process of sanctification. Sanctification is a life-long process of spiritual moral growth of a believer. The process of growth is not completed in the case of most believers. Who can claim that his sanctification (sanctity) has been completed? It is the Holy Spirit of God that sanctifies a believer.

If there is still doubt about this conception of the sacrament, it is hoped that the Apostle Paul's statement in Romans 6:3-4 will dispel the doubt. Paul says, "We are buried with Christ by baptism" (verse 4). How is this saying to be interpreted? It is obvious that this saying is not to be taken literally. In our inquiry of the meaning and the benefits of baptism, other aspects may be uncertain and we are not convinced completely. But there is one aspect we can be certain about. It is that in our Baptism we were not buried with Christ in a real sense. Obviously the apostle Paul used the word "buried" in a figurative sense. This would mean that for Paul baptism is a sign and symbol of what it signifies (its internal meaning) and of the invisible grace of God.

Another example of Paul's use of figurative speech in his teaching about baptism is found in Ephesians 5:25-27. I quote, "Husbands, love your wives just as Christ loved the church and gave himself up for her to make her holy, cleansing her by the washing with water through the word, and to present her to himself as a radiant church, without stain or wrinkle or any other blemish, but holy and blameless." Let us pay attention to the phrase "cleansing her (the church) by the washing with water" (the verse 26). How are we to interpret this phrase? Individual believers are baptized by water. But was there a corporate baptism of a local church also done "by the washing with water"? In the apostolic period, was the local church submerged under water for a corporate baptism? As this is unimaginable, we think that the apostle Paul is using a figure of speech. The church passed with Christ through the baptism of death which he endured on behalf of the church. We recall that Christ himself referred to his death as "baptism" (Mark 10:38-39 and Luke 12:50). Of course, our Lord was speaking figuratively. Christ often used figurative speech. On one occasion he rebuked his disciples for not understanding the meaning of his saying and taking it literally (Matthew 16:5-12).

In Romans 6:3 the apostle Paul also said, "Don't you know that all of us who were baptized into Christ Jesus were baptized unto his death?" "Being baptized into Christ Jesus" – what does this mean? We were baptized into "union with Christ" through the confession of faith in him and the decisive act of commitment to the discipleship of Christ. Indeed Paul says that we were "buried with Christ through baptism in order that, just as Christ was raised from the dead ... we too may live a new life" (verse 4.) Thus baptism is a symbol of death and emergence to a new life; in other words, a symbol of death and resurrection. Union with Christ involved sharing in his death and resurrection. So we conclude that what Paul says in Romans 6:3-4 and in Ephesians 5:25-27 is a figure of speech. This is true of Galatians 3:27 as well. Baptism is a sign and symbol of the invisible grace and of its spiritual benefits. The benefits of baptism, namely, a new life, the forgiveness of sins and the receiving of the gift of the Holy Spirit do not come automatically (*ex opera operato*) from the mere rite of baptism administered by the priest of the church as the Roman Church asserts, but from what take place internally, namely, the believer's repentance, the confession of faith and his decision to become a disciple of Christ. This understanding of baptism is perfectly consistent with the principal line of thought in the New Testament which attaches importance to the internal condition in the heart of a person rather than an external thing like a formal rite of the church.

This principle applies to the sacrament of the eucharist (the Lord's Supper) as well. The Roman doctrine of the sacrament that it works efficaciously *ex opera operato* represents a quite different line of thought which is called "sacrmentalism". But even Peter whom the Roman Church counts on as its patron is not a sacramentalist because he said, "God, who knows the heart, showed that He accepted them (the Gentile Christians) by giving the Holy Spirit to them just as He did to us ... He purified their hearts by faith" (Acts 15:8-9).

The thought that the performance of a prescribed rite by a priest automatically transmits "sacramental grace" is a foreign idea and is incompatible with the Biblical concept of the grace of God. In the Bible the word "grace" means primarily the undeserved favor and loving kindness of God shown to men. In the New Testament "grace" also denotes God's redemptive love. The Catholic doctrine of the sacramental grace ignores the sovereign freedom of the Holy Spirit who works mysteriously. The Catholic doctrine of the *ex opera operato* efficacy of the sacrament presumes that the Holy Spirit works at the bidding of a priest of the church. Is it not a blasphemy to presume that the Holy Spirit works at the bidding of a priest performing a rite? The Scripture teaches that the Holy Spirit works mysteriously (John 3:8) and God dispenses His Spirit "according to His will" (Hebrews 2:4). Is it to be thought that the Sovereign Lord allows a priest of the Roman Church to deprive Him of His sovereign freedom in dispensing His grace? The position of the Roman Church is very difficult to understand. The mere fact that such a position has appeared in a Christian Church is astonishing.

3

The true understanding of the meaning of the sacraments and the proper appraisal of the ecclesiastical, sacramentalist religion of the Roman Church should be sought not only from the biblical passages which refer to the church and the sacraments, but also in the light of the central theological thought of the New Testament. the Scottish theologian Donald Baillie expressed a similar view when he said, "The amount of direct teaching in the New Testament about the sacraments is small, and there is lively controversy in our time as to its real meaning. There are many questions of exegesis that we cannot answer with certainty. Our reconstruction of sacramental theology must rather be based on a deeper understanding of the whole Christian message in the New Testament." We agree with Baillie in this matter. but in the present context of our attempt to make a proper appraisal of the ecclesiastical, sacramentalist religion of the Roman Catholic Church, we found our argument primarily on the theological thought of the fourth gospel and of the apostle Paul, because the Roman Church asserts that its doctrines of the church and the sacrament are based on John 1:14 and Paul's concept of the church as the body of Christ.

"Sacramentalism" does not belong to the central theological thought of either John or Paul, and ecclesiology is not included in the explicit teaching of John's gospel. John does not make a single mention of the church in the gospel. The sacraments and the church are not explicitly described in the proclamation of our Lord. The sacrament had a place in the teaching of our Lord and of his apostles, but it was a matter of a secondary concern for the apostles. The apostle Paul declared, "For Christ did not send me to baptize, but to preach the gospel" (I Corinthians 1:17). Also the apostles themselves rarely administered baptism and usually delegated it to their associates (Acts 1):44-48). In the New Testament a "higher" view of the sacraments has little to build on.

The fourth gospel is a thoroughly theological gospel. It deals with the nature and person of Christ and the meaning of faith in him. John's presentation of Christ as the Son of God is seen in the titles given him in this gospel: "the Word was God"(1:1), "the Lamb of God" (1:29), "the Messiah" (1:40), "the Son of God and the King of Israel" (1:49), "the Savior of the world" (4:42), "the Lord and ... God" (20:28). Christ's deity is asserted in the series of "I am ..." claims (e.g. 8:24, 28, 58). Thus John's statement that "the Word became flesh" (1:14, Incarnation) is one of a series of major theological theses of the fourth gospel. We regard the apostle John as the author of the fourth gospel because the author explicitly says that he is the disciple whom Jesus loved and who was at the Last Supper with Jesus (21:20). He writes that he has witnessed those things written down in the gospel (21:24), and that he is one of those who have personally seens the glory of Jesus (1:14).

Let us consider cautiously how John 1:14 is to be understood, as the Roman Church makes it a foundation of its doctrines of the church and the sacrament. I quote the verse in full:

> *And the Word became flesh, and dwelt among us, and we beheld his glory, glory as of the Only Begotten from the Father, full of grace and truth.*

There is consensus among the exegetes of the fourth gospel that by saying "the Word became flesh", John asserts the genuine humanity of Christ. In the prologue of the gospel (1:1-18) John emphasizes both the deity and the humanity of our Lord. Verse 14 has very rich contents, but the Roman Church concentrated on the word "flesh", stretched its meaning, and reading a preconceived idea into it, interpreted it in a particular direction. It also used Paul's concept of the church as the body of Christ to justify its ecclesiastical, sacramentalist religion. Later it also formed this definition: "the Roman Catholic Church as the Mystical Body of Christ is the extension and continuation of the Incarnation of Christ".

The Roman doctrine that the Roman Church is the mystical body of Christ does not have a biblical basis. Paul used the word "mystery" in reference to the nuptial union of Christ and the church in Ephesians 5:31-32, and not in reference to the church itself. Nowhere in the New Testament is the church called a mystery or mystical. The subtle shift made by the Catholic Church is false. This subtle falsification has been used by the Roman Church to aggrandize itself and its sacraments and hierarchy. This subtle shift is part of the manipulative interpretation of the Holy Scripture which is a habit of the Roman Catholic Church.

In the following I will endeavor to show that an ecclesiastical, sacramentalist religion as found in the Roman Church is not an inherent part of the central theological thought of the apostles John and Paul and is, in all probability, a serious distortion of the Christianity of the New Testament.

The author of the fourth gospel states his purpose in writing the gospel, "These are written that you may believe that Jesus is the Christ, the Son of God, and that by believing you may have life in his name" (20:31). John states a similar theme in 3:16, "God so loved the world that He gave His only Son that whoever believes in him shall not perish but have eternal life." I think that the central thought of John is expressed in this recurrent theme. This theme resounds in the First Epistle of John as well (4:9-10). Moreover John 3:16 is, along with 3:14-15, a quotation of Christ's own saying. So it is even weightier. There is not the slightest indication of an ecclesiastical, sacramentalist religion in the recurrent theme of the gospel according to John. Therefore we question the way the Catholic Church deals with the phrase in John 1:14, "the Word became flesh," as if it were the central, main theme of John's gospel, and uses it to support its ecclesiocentric, sacramentalist religion.

Based on John 1:14, which refers to the Incarnation of Christ, the orthodox Catholic theologians argue roughly as follows. It is inconceivable that the Incarnate Christ who came to the human world on earth stayed for a brief period of time and withdrew, leaving behind no more than his memory. The Incarnation must be made present and extended even after Christ ascended to heaven. Therefore the Church as the continuation and extension of the Incarnation is required. Indeed the Roman Church as the Mystical Body of Christ has taken the place of the Incarnate Christ. Thus a theological foundation for the Catholic Church's self-glorification has been laid.

This argument may sound plausible and persuasive. But no matter how plausible it may be, it is a speculative theory made by humans and is not solidly based on the biblical teaching. It lacks plain biblical evidence. That the Roman Church teaches such a doctrine indicates that it has not paid careful attention to what is written in the Scripture, because a crucial passage in John's gospel denies that Christ has simply withdrawn from this world and left behind no more than his memory. According to John, Christ said that his departure was rather "to the advantage" of Christian people because he was going to send the Holy Spirit for them after he had gone. Christ said this during the Last Supper with his disciples:

But I tell you the truth, it is to your advantage that I go away;
for if I do not go away, the Helper shall not come to you; but
if I go I will send Him to you ...

<John 16:7>

"The Helper" refers to the Holy Spirit (cf. 15:26; 7:39). The meaning of these words of Christ, which were emphatically and plainly stated, is clear and unequivocal. I think that these words of the Incarnate Christ invalidate the Catholic interpretation of the Incarnation of Christ which has become the basis of the Catholic doctrine of the Church as the continuation and extension of the Incarnation. The meaning conveyed in John 16:7 is that Christ would not leave the believers in a state like that of orphans (John 14:18), but that His presence with believers would be through the Holy Spirit he was going to send, not through the Roman Catholic Church which is falsely alleged to be the continuation and extension of the Incarnation. "The extension of the Incarnation" can be rephrased as "the extension of the Incarnate Christ."

Here we focus on the Catholic doctrine that the Roman Church is the continuation of the Incarnation of Christ. The fact that the Catholic Church has made and teaches the doctrine means that the Roman Church disregarded and paid no attention to the words of Christ in John 16:7, namely that his withdrawal was to the advantage of believers and he would send the Holy Spirit for them. If the Catholic Church ignores the saying of Christ (John 16:7), then why does it not ignore the saying of John 1:14, "The Word became flesh"? The Roman Church has to either believe both John 1:14 and 16:7 or disbelieve both. This is a forced option. In either choice, the Catholic Church's astounding claim that it is the continuation and extension of the Incarnation of Christ is made invalid.

Conclusion

The Christian Church and individual Christians should believe both John 1:14 and 16:7. In other words, we should believe the Incarnation of the Word (Christ) and also believe the words of the Incarnate Word that Christ's withdrawal from the earth was for the greater good of the Church because after he ascended to heaven he would send the Holy Spirit for us, and because his promise has been kept. From the exalted Christ, the Holy Spirit came to be the life and guide of the Church until Christ's return in glory at the end of the world. Accordingly, the claim of the Roman Church that the Catholic Church is the continuation of the Incarnation, and that it takes the place of the Incarnate Christ after his ascension to heaven reveals its ignoring of Christ's words. Of course the Roman Church believes that the Holy Spirit has come and is at work in the Church, and it says so. But does the Roman Church know that the Holy Spirit has come and has, in effect, taken the place of the Incarnate Christ who has ascended to heaven? If the Catholic Church does not know this it is strange, because John 16:7 clearly indicates this. If the Roman Catholic Church knows it and yet still claims that it is the continuation of the Incarnate Christ, then it is even more strange because this claim contradicts John 16:7. As the Holy Spirit has come and is in place of the Incarnate Christ, there is no need of the continuation of the Incarnate Christ. The Roman Church's dubious claim was deduced by logical inference. Its logical inference is not so logical after all.

I do not know how the Catholic Church will extricate itself from this dilemma. We remind ourselves and the magisterium of the Catholic Church that what concerns the saving acts of God cannot be fully. Comprehended by human logic. The subject matter is far beyond the capacity of our feeble human logic and it is far too profound to be handled by humans by means of mere logic. This is the reason why God has provided for His people with the Holy Scripture, which has its own logic. Jesus said,

I praise You, Father, Lord of heaven and earth, because You have hidden these things from the wise and learned, and revealed them to little children. Yes, Father, for this was Your good pleasure.
<Matthew 11:25-26>

I quote Isaiah 34:16 of the Old Testament.

Seek and read from the book of the Lord: Not one of these shall be missing; none shall be without her mate. For the mouth of the Lord has commanded, and His Spirit has gathered them.

"The book of Lord" refers to the Holy Scripture.

God Who has provided beautiful nature for our eyes to see, and beautiful music for our ears to hear, has provided the Holy Scripture for our soul as spiritual food for the eternal life.

4

The Apostle Paul's central theological thought is expounded rather systematically in two of his epistles, namely, Romans and Galatians. Neither the church nor the sacraments hold any place in Paul's central thought. Paul's primary theme in Romans is the basic gospel, God's plan of salavation and righteousness for all mankind (1:16-17). Paul's thought is expounded in the framework of the salvation history of God. The main themes which constitute his central thought are God's grace and love, redemption through the atoning death of Christ on the cross, reconciliation, and justification by faith through grace rather than by keeping the law given through Moses. "Justification" means, for Paul, "being declared as righteous" by God. The core of Paul's central theological thought is expressed in Romans 3:20-24:

> By the works of the Law no one will be justified in His sight; for through the Law comes the knowledge of sin. But now apart from the Law the righteousness of God has been manifested, being witnessed by the Law and the prophets; even the righteousness of God through faith in Jesus Christ for all those who believe; for there is no distinction; for all have sinned and fall short of the glory of God, being justified as a gift by His grace through the redemption which is in Christ Jesus.

Paul's antithesis between the law (which came through Moses) and grace (which has come through Christ) is expressed in these few verses. For Paul, reconciliation (the restoration of the right relationship with God), the forgiveness of sin, and justification mean largely the same thing. Paul says, "God demonstrates His own love toward us, in that while we were yet sinners, Christ died for us" (Romans 5:8). Paul's theme expressed here is the same in essence as John's recurrent theme which we have noted above.

Sin is not merely a stain or corruption of the soul. It is much more than that. Sin is an offence against God, causing the rupture of the relationship with God. The ruptured relationship is restored only through the atonement of sin by Christ's death on the cross which was achieved by God's own initiative. Thus a believer's reconciliation with God and justification (being regarded as righteous) are obtained by the grace of God. A believer is not only justified but also sanctified by faith through the grace of God. In a believer's sanctification the Holy Spirit participates and plays an essential part.

The Roman Catholic Church shows a lack of understanding of Paul's central thought presented in Paul's epistles to the Romans and the Galatians. As a matter of fact the Roman Church has ignored the two epistles. But Paul's central thought reverberates even in the epistles to the Corinthians, the Ephesians and the Colossians, which are highly valued by the Catholic Church because the references to the church are made in them. The passages in these epistles which echo Paul's central theme are I Corinthians 1:17-24, 30, 2:1-2; II Corinthians 5:19-21, 14-15; Ephesians 2:6-8; Colossians 1:14, 20-22. Paul's doctrine of salvation by the grace of God conforms to the fundamental proclamation of Christ which is expounded in, for example, two of his parables, namely, the Parable of the Laborers in the Vineyard (Matthew 20:1-16), and the Parable of the Pharisees and the Publican (Luke 17:9-14). Paul recognized that this concept of grace is central to the gospel of Christ. It is no little matter that the Roman Catholic Church has failed to grasp this gospel of our Lord.

Paul does not mention "the church" in his lengthy discussion of what we regard as his central thought in Romans. The word "church" is conspicuously absent from 15 long chapters (the 1st to 15th). Only in the 16th chapter which is the last of the epistle, the word church is mentioned in connection with his greeting to dozens of individual believers. A similar phenomenon is found in the epistle to the Galatians. This fact would seem to be part of the reason that the Catholic Church neglects these two epistles. The main reason is that Paul's central theme presented in them is incompatible with Roman Catholicism. There is a fundamental theological difference between the two. It is to be noted that even Peter whom the Catholic Church counts on as its patron echoes Paul's central theme. More accurately, it was Peter's own faith and preaching theme which was delivered using different expression. Cf. Acts 15:9-11; I Peter 2:24. If "the church" was to become such an all-important central entity in Christianity as the Roman Church makes out, it is difficult to explain the fact that Paul does not mention the church in his presentation of his central thought and that the gospels of Mark, Luke and John do not make a single explicit reference to it.

In the foregoing we saw that "the church" is not mentioned explicitly in the central thought of John and Paul. Neither is it in Jesus' proclamation. Yet the Roman Catholic Church established an ecclesiocentric, sacramentalist religion based on a peculiar interpretation of John 1:14, "the Word became flesh," and of Paul's saying in Ephesians 4:12 "the church is the body of Christ." This is an illegitimate procedure. We have endeavored to demonstrate that this ecclesiocenric religion is incompatible with the central and fundamental theology of John and Paul, and with the proclamation of the Lord Himself.

But if "the church" is clearly conceived as "the people of God", then it is admitted that the preciousness of the church is assumed from the beginning to the end in the theologies of John and Paul and in the New Testament, for the people of God (the church) is the very object of God's love and the very purpose of God's redemptive enterprise. But no matter how precious and beloved the church may be in the eyes of God, God's saving acts and undeserved mercy and grace for the fallen humans are the main theme of the apostolic preaching and writing.

The reason I emphasized that "the church" is not even mentioned by John and Paul in the presentation of their central thought is to dispute the pretentious place assigned to the church in the ecclesio-centric religion of the Roman Church. I give two quotations from The Catechism of the Catholic Church for illustration.

"Outside the Church there is no salvation." ... means that all salvation comes from Christ the Head through the Church which is his Body.

<No. 846>

Where there is Christ Jesus, there is the Catholic Church. In her subsists the fullness of Christ's body united with its head; this implies that she received from him "fullness of the means of salvation" which he has willed.

<No.830>

We reject the Catholic Church's such self-understanding and self-importance as biblically unwarranted. Let us briefly consider the apostle Paul's concept of the church.

5

In I Corinthians 1:2-3, Paul's concept of the church is typically expressed, "To the church of God in Corinth, to those sanctified in Christ Jesus and called to be holy, together with those everywhere who call on the name of our Lord Jesus Christ ... Grace and peace to you from God our Father and the Lord Jesus Christ." In Paul's two epistles to the Corinthians the church is "a local congregation" (as it is in Acts, James, John's third epistle and Revelation). But every local congregation is "the church of God" (I Corinthians 1:2). The local congregation represents the church of God; it is the local representation of the universal church of Christ. Also every local congregation is the church of God in the sense of being the people of God who call on the name of the Lord Jesus Christ. Probably Paul's concept of the church as "the body of Christ" is to be understood from this perspective because Paul says to the believers in Corinth, "You are the body of Christ and each one of you is a part of it" (I Corinthians 12:27). So the church is not an institution, but the people of God. If this understanding is correct, it means that the Roman Catholic Church's doctrine of the church as the mystical body of Christ and the hierarchical community is quite remote from Paul's own modest concept. Paul's saying to the Christian congregation in Corinth, "You are the body of Christ and each one of you is a part of it," is to be taken as a figure of speech (as he often uses it elsewhere). If it is taken literally, it is absurd and creates enormous difficulty.

If taken literally, then each member of the congregation (church) in Corinth is a part of the body of Christ. Does this make sense? Evidently this is a nonsensical notion. It is also a serious departure from Paul's central thought and his concept of the church mentioned above. Yet the Roman Church seems to interpret Paul's saying almost literally and asserts that, together with John 1:14, Paul's teaching is the basis of the Catholic doctrine of the church. I remind our Catholic friends that the use of a figure of speech is a quite common practice in the Holy Scripture. Even God Almighty used parables and figures of speech. God said, "I spoke to the prophets, gave them many visions and told parables through them" (Hosea 12:10).

I give examples:

The Lord said, "You yourselves have seen what I did to the Egyptians, and how I carried you on eagles' wings and brought you here to Myself."
<Exodus 19:4>

"Come now and let us reason together," says the Lord, "Though your sins are as scarlet, they will be as white as snow; though they are as red like crimson, and they will be like wool."
<Isaiah 1:18>

Our Lord Jesus Christ also told many parables. In Matthew 13:34 we read,

Jesus spoke all these things to the crowd in parables, and he did not say anything to them without using a parable.

To be sure, the magisterium of the Roman Church knows this. Yet it picked out a few out of many figures of speech and interpreted them literally when it perceived that they suited its purpose. This is an arbitrary and manipulative interpretation of the Scripture.

For the apostle Paul the church is "the bride of Christ" as well (Ephesians 5:25-32; II Corinthians 11:2). This phrase too is to be taken as a figure of speech, just as the people of Israel was called "the wife of the Lord" in the Old Testament and that was taken as a figure of speech. The church as the bride of Christ must be a humble people of God rather than an authoritarian, triumphant, ecclesiastic government. The humble people of God who "call on the name of our Lord Jesus Christ" is a perfect image of the church as the bride of Christ.

The church as the people of God has a counterpart in the Old Testament. God said to the Israelites through Moses, "Then I will take you for My people, and I will be your God; and you shall know that I am the Lord your God" (Exodus 6:7). In the 13th chapter of Ezekiel, God uses the expression "My people" seven times. In that chapter God also condemns the false prophets who deceived and misled the people of Israel, and declared, "I will deliver My people out of your hands" (verses 21 and 23). God also said elsewhere, "Behold, I am against those who have prophesied false dreams and related them, and led My people astray by their falsehoods and reckless boasting; yet I did not send them or command them" (Jeremiah 23:32).

According to the prophets of God, God laments the gullibility and blind submission of His people to wicked religious leaders and false prophets (Jeremiah 5:31; Ezekiel 13:19). Gullibility and blind submission are not praiseworthy. God condemned the religious leaders who misled the people by "falsehoods and reckless boasting". He said, "I did not send or command them." Such false leaders abounded in the Middle Ages and they exist in our own times as well.

In the New Testament, the church as the bride of Christ is the primary analogy (figure of speech) whereas the church as the body of Christ is the secondary analogy. When the primary analogy is pushed aside and a secondary analogy becomes dominant, it means not merely that the primary analogy fell into neglect, but also that the truth is being distorted. This distortion of truth has taken place in the Roman Catholic Church. The Roman Church has exalted itself by a self-serving procedure and inordinate exaggeration, and it has established an authoritarian ecclesio-centric religion. As a result the New Testament teaching about the church as the bride of Christ and the people of God has been obscured. The primacy of the nuptial analogy (the church as the bride) is consistent with the fact that Christianity is a personalist religion.

The Roman Church formed its doctrine of the church as the "mystical" body of Christ based on St. Paul's teaching by analogy in Ephesians 5:31-32 and it neglected Paul's primary analogy of the bride of Christ in favor of the analogy of the body of Christ, which suited its purpose.

Is there biblical basis for the assertion that the analogy of the bride of Christ is primary and the analogy of the body of Christ is secondary? Certainly! Here is an indisputable fact which everyone who studies the Holy Scripture can ascertain for himself. The analogy of bride-bridegroom, wife-husband is frequently used in the Old and the New Testaments, whereas the analogy of the body of Christ is found in the epistles of Paul only. I give an example. The prophet Hosea portrayed God as husband Israel as erring wife.

> *"And I will betroth you to Me forever, Yes, I will betroth you to Me in righteousness and in justice, in loving kindness and in compassion. And I will betroth you to Me in faithfulness ...,"* *declares the Lord.*
>
> <Hosea 2:19-20>

The prophet Isaiah also depicts the relationship between God and Israel as that between bridegroom and bride (Isaiah 62:5).

Most important is the fact that Christ himself frequently used the nuptial analogy, e.g. Matthew 25:1-13, 22:1-3, 9:15. Also he performed his first miracle at a wedding feast in Cana of Galilee by changing water into wine to help the celebration of the wedding. In the last two chapters of Revelation the church is still called "a bride". The Holy Scripture employs the marriage analogy as a figure of speech for the covenant relation between God and His people. The relation between the husband and the wife and the relation between God and His people are regarded as analogous covenant relations (Ezekiel 16:8, 60; Malachi 2:14-15).

These biblical accounts reinforce the theological proposition that the God testified in the Scripture is "a personal God" and the biblical religion is "a personalist religion". This personalist religion stands in a sharp contrast with the ecclesiastical, sacramentalist, ritualist religion of the Roman Catholic Church which effectively "depersonalizes" the Christianity of the New Testament.

Here we come back to Paul's concept of the church; it is to be noted that Paul makes a clear distinction between the ministers (of the church) and the church as the people of God. See Acts 20:17-31, especially verse 28. A similar distinction was made by God in the Old Testament between the prophets and priests on the one hand and the people of God on the other (Jeremiah 8:10-11). It seems that making this distinction was a common practice in the days of the apostles. See Acts 15:4 and 22. In this respect, too, the doctrine of the Catholic Church differs from the New Testament. In The Catechism of the Catholic Church we read,

> The Church is both visible and spiritual, a hierarchical society and the Mystical Body of Christ.
>
> <No. 779>

> ... the Church acts in the sacraments as "an organically structured priestly community"
>
> <No. 1119>

I also quote the pope Pius XI's encyclical Quas primas(1925), in which he declared that the Church "not only symbolizes the definitive reign of God over the universe, but actuates, if gradual degrees, the sovereignty of Christ in the world ..." The Catholic theologian Robert Bellarmine(S.J) defined the Church as "the society of Christian believers united in the profession of the one Christian faith and the participation in the one sacramental system under the government of the Roman Pontiff." Bellarmine was elevated to the rank of "Doctor of the Church" by the pope Pius XI in 1930.

This discrepancy, like many others, points in the same direction, demonstrating the questionableness of the Catholic doctrines of the church and the hierarchy, and ultimately the questionableness of the Roman Catholic Church. In the Catholic Church the church is "idolized". But the apostle Peter whom the Catholic Church regards as its patron said, "it is time for judgement to begin with the household of God." (The first epistle of Peter 4:17) "The household of God" refers to the church.

6

Here we return to our main theme, the apostle Paul's central theological thought. Paul's theme which places emphasis on the grace of God resounds in John's gospel as well. In 1:16-17 John say:

From His fullness we have all received grace upon grace.
For the Law was given through Moses; grace and truth came
through Jesus Christ.

John's theme expressed here is identical with Paul's theme presented in Romans 3:20-24. There is a striking parallel and similarity between the two. This theme of John resounds in the verse as well which is regarded as the crucial by the Roman Church, namely, John 1:14 I quote it again:

The World became flesh, and dwelt among us,
and we beheld His glory, glory as of the Only
Begotten from the Father, full of grace and truth.

The words of Christ in John 5:45 are in accord with this Pauline-Johannine theme. Christ said to the Jews, "Do not think that I will accuse you before the Father. Your accuser is Moses." The biblical commentator T.F. Elassen has written a book to show that the contrast of Moses and Christ is one of John's major themes (Moses in the Fourth gospel. London, 1963). John said, "the law was given through Moses; grace and truth came through Christ" (1:17). Thus John associates both grace and truth with the gospel of Jesus Christ. John's concern is with the new way of salvation by grace as it is revealed and established through Christ. This new way of salvation by grace is the truth; it is the truth of the gospel.

In the foregoing I have made critical appraisals of the Roman Church's particular interpretation of the Incarnation of Christ spoken of in John 1:14, and of the way the Catholic Church uses that interpretation to legitimize its doctrines of the church, the sacraments, and its ecclesiastical, sacramentalist religion.

Here I add one more critical comment. John 1:15 has rich contents as we have already noted earlier. But the Roman Church focused on one word "flesh" and formulated, by logical inference, its grandiose doctrines of the church and the sacrament, neglecting the rest of the contents of the verse. Let us pay attention to its contents. I quote John 1:14 again.

The Word became flesh and dwelt among us.
And we beheld His glory, glory as of the Only
Begotten from the Father, full of grace and truth.

The image of Christ portrayed briefly in this verse by John the eyewitness, is that of the glorious and gracious Son of God. It matches the testimonies given in the four gospels which show Christ as the mighty and gracious Messiah who performed a large number of astonishing miracles and rose again from the dead. The gospels also show Christ as the gracious, tender friend of sinners and outcasts of society who are despised and rejected by the religious establishment. He sat at table with sinners, visited sinner's home, fed the hungry, healed the sick and taught the common people. The figure of Christ given in the gospels is the merciful Savior who came to call sinners to repentance and offered this invitation, "Come to me, all you who are weary and burdened, and I will give you rest" (Matthew 11:28). Christ in the gospels is anything but the severe, merciless Judge, whom "the Virgin Mary" his mother tries, often in vain, to move to have compassion. According to the Marian cult in the Catholic Church, the Virgin Mary pleads with her Son on behalf of the believers who appeal to her for help. The pope John Paul II also publicly expressed his devotion to Mary during his reign.

Conclusion

The Roman Church's interpretation of John 1:14 is one sided and fails to give the true figure of Christ, thus failing to do justice to Christ himself. This Christ as a tender gracious living Person is not well harmonized with the impersonal character of the ecclesiastical, sacramentalist religion of the Roman Catholic Church. What we call "the personalist religion" which characteristically represents New Testament Christianity is far better harmonized with his figure of Christ given in John's gospel and the Synoptic gospels.

John and Paul are similar in another respect, namely that they present their central theological thought in the framework of the salvation history of God. Paul's salvation-historical viewpoint is most clearly expressed in his two speeches recorded in Acts 24:10-21 and 26:1-23.

The crucial point here in the context of our debate with Romeo is that John conceives of the Incarnation of Christ clearly in the framework of the salvation history, consistent with his central thought. What does this mean? It means that the Roman Church's ecclesiastical, sacramentalist interpretation of the incarnation is not in accord with John's central thought, nor with Paul's. If this observation is true, the ecclesiastical, sacramentalist religion of the Roman Catholic Church will suffer a blow since the Roman Church claims that its doctrines of the church and the sacrament are based on John 1:14 and on Paul's teaching that the church is the body of Christ.

In order to reinforce our argument, I point out that our Lord Jesus too understood his redemptive work from the perspective of God's salvation history as recorded in the Old Testament. He said:

Just as Moses lifted up the snake in the desert,
so the Son of Man must be lifted up, that whoever
believes in him may have eternal life.
<John 3:14-15>

This statement refers to the account recorded in Numbers 21:4-9. In addition Luke 24:25-27, 44-48 clearly demonstrates that Jesus and Zechariah, the father of John the Baptist, also understood the things that happened to them from the viewpoint of God's salvation history. Cf. Luke 1:47-55; 1:67-79. The Roman Church which teaches its members to venerate Mary greatly would do well to keep this in mind. Actually the salvation history of God represents the perspective of the entire New Testament. Cf. Luke 9:28-30; Mark 9:2-4; Hebrew 1:1-3.

It will be difficult for the magisterium of the Catholic Church to claim that the ecclesiocentric, sacramentalist religion of the Roman Church also has its background firmly in salvation history. If the magisterium claims so, it is not justified and will not be able to substantiate the claim. The salvation history of God recorded in the Scripture is a reality that the Church of Rome has failed to fully recognize clearly, let alone do full justice to it. This is not strange in view of the fact that the pope and the papal court have not treated the Holy Scripture with proper respect since the early Middle Ages.

The distinguished Catholic theologian Karl Rahner frankly admitted that Catholic theology has neglected salvation history. I quote him again, "This theology of the phases of God's plan of salvation is the proper task for the systematic theology of history … Catholic theology, to be sure, has not yet addressed itself to this task."

I point to the Roman Catholic dogma of "tradition" as an illustration of what kind of treatment the Scripture has received in the Roman Church. The dogma gave the tradition in the Catholic Church a status equal to the Holy Scripture as a source of revelation. I will deal with this Catholic dogma separately in Appendix C. The Roman Church has not in practice treated the Scripture with due respect. There has been this tendency in the Roman Church since its beginning. I quote the church historian Adolf Harnack again. " …in Rome theology never flourished, either in antiquity or in the Middle Ages. There was practical concern in Rome neither with Scripture exposition nor with the dogmatic works of the Fathers. Whoever wished to study theology went to France. For the curia, only the student of law was of any account." As another illustration of the Roman Church's insufficient respect shown to the Holy Scripture. I point to the fact, the Thomas Aquinas, the angelic doctor of the Roman Church, disregarded a divine command which strictly forbids syncretism and any transaction with pagan thought, and idolized Aristotle, a pagan philosopher, as "the Philosopher" and attempted to synthesize Christian theology and Aristotelian philosophy, and to the fact that the Roman Church idolized Thomas as "the theologian" and formally endorsed Thomism. Therefore what God proclaimed through the prophet Jeremiah has relevance in this case:

> *"They have spurned the word of the Lord, and what*
> *sort of wisdom is theirs? ... says the Lord."*
> <8:9, 12>

Accordingly we cannot free ourselves of the feeling that it is no wonder that the Roman Catholic Church has transmuted into an ecclesiastical, sacramentalist religion which is a perversion of the Christianity of the New Testament.

Earlier I have discussed the Catholic church's disregard of Christ's saying recorded in John 16:7 and the disastrous consequence. I continue to discuss the Catholic Church's seemingly only lukewarm belief in Christ's teaching about the authority and importance of the Holy Scripture. Of course the magisterium of the Roman Church asserts that it believes every word Christ has spoken and accepts the authority of the Scripture. But we suspect that what the magisterium says is one thing and what it practices is another. Its habit of manipulative interpretation of the Scripture is an indication of this. The Catholic dogma of tradition is another. The fact that the Roman Church teaches doctrines and practices which do not have a sound biblical basis is still another. Revealed in these practices is the Roman Church's virtual ignoring of our Lord's teaching about the Scripture and its disobedience to him. I have repeatedly pointed out the Catholic Church's disregard of the words of our Lord in John

16:7. If it followed them, it would not be able to claim that the Roman Catholic Church is the extension and continuation of the Incarnation of Christ. These practices of the Roman Catholic Church are also in breach of the instruction of the apostle Paul. The apostle said:

> *Now, brothers, I have applied these things to myself*
> *and Apollos for your benefit, so that you may learn*
> *from us the meaning of the saying, "Do not go beyond what*
> *is written."*
> <I Corinthians 4:6>

What the Church of Christ should do is not to make new doctrines by "logical inference" or by "the infallible teaching authority" allegedly bestowed on it by Christ, but rather, "contend for the faith that God has once for all entrusted to the saints" (Jude verse 3). "The faith that God has once for all entrusted to the saints" is deposited in the Holy Scripture. The pope's claim to be "the infallible teaching authority" has no biblical basis. I will deal with this presumptuous claim in Appendix D. I wonder if the pope's presumptuous claims including this one are comparable with "falsehoods and reckless boasting" of the false prophets condemned by God (Jeremiah 23:32).

The respect Christ had for the Scripture (the Old Testament) is evident in all four gospels. I give a few passages as examples: Matthew 4:4-11, 22:29; Luke 24:25-27, 44-47; John 5:39, 10:35, 13:18, 17:12. The attitude Christ had for the Scripture is no less important for us than his words. Should not the Christian Church and the Christian people follow the example of Christ in this? The Roman Church has demanded the obedience of every Catholic, asserting that the obedience to Christ must be the obedience to their Church, and obedience to the Church must be the obedience to the pope. This has been a persistent demand. The obedience to the Church is held to be meritorious for salvation. Popes have even declared that no one that does not submit to the pope will be saved. But popes themselves and the Roman Church itself have been disobedient or only half-heartedly obedient to Christ as far as their practices regarding the Holy Scripture is concerned. The Catholic Church's disobedience to Christ in this respect will be discussed in some detail in Appendix C.

There is an apparent inconsistency between the two different attitudes taken by the Roman Church to the Holy Scripture. On the one hand there was for a long time no "practical concern" in Rome with the Scripture and theology (in the words of Adolf Harnack). On the other hand the magisterium of the Catholic Church formulated its doctrines based on texts of the Scripture. But in reality this is merely a seeming inconsistency because the magisterium did not first listen with due respect, as it should, to what the biblical text says and then formulate the doctrines accordingly, but rather it read its preconceived ideas into the text in order to legitimize the existent ecclesiastic institution of the Roman Church. Its use of John 1:14 and Matthew 16:18 are the most conspicuous examples. As mentioned repeatedly, John 1:14 is used to legitimize the self-aggrandizing Catholic Church, and Matt. 16:18 the papal claim to supremacy. If the Holy Scripture is "used" by the magisterium of the Roman Church or by anyone to legitimize the existent system, it is not only a disrespectful attitude shown to the Scripture, but also a blasphemy against the word of God in the Scripture.

7

The doctrine of the church is fundamental to one's understanding of the Roman Catholic Church. Developed down the centuries, it bears the marks of the Middle Ages when the imperial background influenced the conception of the church as an imperium, with a resultant stress on the ecclesiastic structure and organization, on the hierarchy and its power, and on the claims of the monarchical pope. This is a heritage of the ancient Romans who conceived Christianity and the church in legalistic terms and exerted influence on the way of thinking and on the development of the polity of the Catholic Church. So it is no surprise that the Church has come to have the name of the "Roman" Catholic Church.

Then how did this happen? How was it justified? It was asserted that the Catholic Church was founded by Christ and was endowed with the authority to teach the saving truth of God and to celebrate the sacraments which dispense the saving grace essential for salvation. So the priesthood is required for teaching and celebrating the sacraments. Thus the institution of the priesthood is justified. The celebration of the sacraments is tied to the order of the clergy whom Christ has appointed. At the same time this order alone is alleged to have been authorized to interpret the law of Christ with binding authority. Therefore everyone must submit to the clergy. Thus a strict distinction between the clergy and the lay people came to be made.

As salvation is a mystery that cannot be "experienced" in the ordinary sense of the word and no one can have a certainty regarding his salvation The only way left for the believer is to surrender himself to the sacramental saving system in the Roman Church which was allegedly provided by God. Not being saved meant going to hell for everlasting punishment. In this way the absolute authority of the Catholic Church and its clergy was established.

It was also asserted that the Bishop of Rome, the pope, is the chief of the clergy and the supreme head of the universal Church in the world because he alone is allegedly the successor of Peter whom Christ appointed to be the prince of the apostles. Accordingly all humans, including kings and emperors, must submit to the pope. Thus the institution of the papacy was legitimized and came to be aggrandized. The papacy and Church were inseparably tied together.

In the Middle Ages it was natural for people to be concerned about thir salvation in the next world after death and greatly to fear eternal punishment in hell. There was a general agreement that if a person is to be saved he must receive the divine grace which is dispensed through the sacraments. As the intermediary between God and man and as the authorized dispenser of sacramental grace, the Roman Church was recognized by most people as indispensable. As long as this fundamental conception of salvation and blessedness was accepted and every believer needed to avail himself of the sacraments, the authority of the Church as the sacramental saving institution and the status of the priest were secure. It was this common belief among people that gave the Church its hold on them, enabling it to keep them docile and making them loyal to the Church. But this impressive sacramental system of the Roman Church had a grievous "side effect." As it was taught by the Church and was accepted by people that the sacraments of the Church are effective *ex opere operato* (automatically so to speak) in dispensing the divine grace *for salvation*, the sacramental system produced a false sense of security and complacency among the people as if their salvation were now a secure possession.

Although in the Middle Ages the authority of the Catholic Church had been firmly established, no doctrine of the church was officially formulated and promulgated. But the ambitious, powerful popes such as Gregory VII (1073-1085), Innocent III (1198-1216) and Boniface VIII (1294-1303) made claims to supremacy not only on the entire Christian Church, but also over the nations of the earth. The emergence of the pope to such a political eminence and power was achieved, initially, by the pope's severance of the relationship with the Roman emperor in Byzantium, which was called New Roman or the Second Rome after the transfer of the capital of the empire from Rome to Byzantium in the East by the emperor Constantine in the 4th century. Byzantium was renamed by the emperor as Constantinople. The pope who assumed the new leadership role in Old Rome engaged in a political coalition with the enemies of the Roman Empire, namely, the rulers of the Franks-Germanics (the barbarian tribes in the West). The pope presumed, on his own authority, to confer the title of emperor on a Germanic prince named Charlemagne in 800 A.D. From Byzantium's standpoint such a development in the West was a joint rebellion of the bishop of Rome (the pope) and the Western barbarian princes, who reciprocally appropriated to themselves power positions and legal titles to which they could lay no legitimate claims. The pope's authority and power in the West were established in the church first, and then his political stature also rose so high that even the emperor had to respect the pope's position.

The pope's political ascendancy in the West was accelerated

by the use of a forged document (The Donation of Constantine) that granted the papacy territorial rights to much of Western world. This document attempted to reconstruct the history of the Roman papacy in order to legitimize the newly gained ecclesiastical and political stature of the popes after the disappearance of the Roman imperial reign in the West. According to this document the emperor Constantine transferred the capital to Byzantium so that the power of the Bishop of Rome should not be limited by the presence of the emperor in Rome. On the basis of this forged document, the bishop of Rome, the pope, could legitimately take over the vast lands and all the legal functions of the Roman emperor. The Donation of Constantine was generally accepted as a genuine document and was effectively used by the pope and papalists. It was not until the 15th century that scholars demonstrated that it was a forgery. By then the immense political power and the vast territories were already in the hands of the pope. The principal architects of the papal theory of the Middle Ages were not theologians, but canon lawyers (papal lawyers). Centuries have passed. In time theologians worked out elaborate theories to legitimize theologically the existing church and the papacy by means of manipulative interpretation of biblical passages. As I have already mentioned, John 1:14 and Paul's concept of the church as the body of Christ were used as the main biblical basis of the doctrine of the church, and Matthew 16:18 for the doctrine of the papal primacy.

8

The foregoing is a brief summary of the Catholic doctrines of the church, the sacraments, the priest and the papacy. But they do not have a sound biblical basis. rather they contradict the fundamental teaching of the New Testament that thanks to Christ's atoning death, free access is open to the throne of grace and no human intermediary is needed between God and the believer (Hebrews 4:16). The Epistle to the Hebrews is devoted to expound this fundamental truth. Jesus offered himself on the cross as the sacrifice for the redemption of mankind. In that sense Christ is a Priest. He is "a Priest forever" who offered "one sacrifice for sins for all time" (Hebrews 7:21, 10:21). Thus the sacrifice was offered "once for all" and completed by Christ. The "once-for-all-ness" of the sacrifice is emphasized (Hebrews 9:12, 26, 28; 10:10 and 12). Therefore there is no need of any more sacrifice and no need of any other priest. This is the fundamental teaching of Hebrews. The apostles Peter and Paul also taught the once-for-all-ness of Christ's sacrificial death (I Peter 3:18; Romans 6:10).

The Roman Church's doctrines of the eucharist (the mass) as "sacrifice" and of the clergy as "priest" contradict this teaching. Likewise the Catholic doctrines of the church and the priest also contradict the plainest words of Christ, e.g. John 3:16 and the Parable of the Prodigal Son (Luke 15:11-32). It is doubtful that the Roman doctrine of sacramental grace has a solid biblical basis.

In the theology of the New Testament which teaches free direct access to the gracious God through Jesus Christ, there is no room for a human priest or the sacrament of penance which is held to dispense sacramental grace, namely, the absolution of sins and of punishment in hell. The Lord's Prayer also teaches direct access to God. Our Lord taught us to say, "Our Father who art in heaven," and to ask for the forgiveness of sin directly, "Forgive us our debts as we also have forgiven our debtors." Implied in this petition is that our heavenly Father forgives our sins without any human intermediary like the priest or the rite called the sacrament of penance, just as we (can) forgive our fellow humans who have done wrongs to us.

Let us consider the Parable of the Prodigal Son. In this parable Jesus likens the relationship between God and the sinner to that between a human father and his prodigal son who left home and squandered the father's wealth in dissipation. In the restoration of the relationship between father and son, it is evident that there was no mediator needed because when the son returned home to his father in repentance, the father embraced and kissed him and received him back. The father even gave a sumptuous party to celebrate the son's home-coming. According to this parable, in the restoration of the relationship between God and the repentant sinner, there is no need of a human priest or a ceremonial rite. Having said this, I hasten to add that in the Gospel preached by Jesus and in the New Testament Jesus' essential role as the God-sent mediator through his atoning death is strongly emphasized (e.g. John 14:6, 3:16; Romans 5:8-11, II Corinthians 5:18-20; Hebrews 4:14-16, 7:25, 9:11-15, 10:19). In the Gospel of Jesus Christ God has opened up a new and living way into His presence, making His mercy free to all who repent and believe. Therefore in this Parable of the Prodigal Son too Jesus' mediatorial role is assumed although it is not mentioned. Other than Jesus, no human intermediary is needed. God is accessible to the sinner directly when he repents and returns to God. Thus, in this parable the relationship of the repentant sinner to God is described as a personal relationship. The human priest as an intermediary between God and man is a presumptuous intrusion. Nowhere in the New Testament do we find the idea that the eucharist is a sacrifice or that the minister of the church is a "priest". There are rather passages in the New Testament which can be taken as contrary evidence to the idea (e.g. I Corinthians 12:28-30; Ephesians 4:11-12). Not once is the word "priest" used of the minister of the church in the New Testament. Not once is the church regarded as the priestly hierarchical institution.

Furthermore there is no historical evidence that in the apostolic period the ministers of the church were called or regarded as priests. The practice of calling the minister a priest emerged in the churches only after the apostles had died. I maintain the proposition presented above and assert that it can be verified biblically and historically. We cannot free ourselves of the suspicion that the self-aggrandizing church and the sacramental system of the Roman Catholic Church came to exist partly due to historical and cultural circumstances, and partly due to the misunderstanding of the biblical teaching, but mainly due to the desire of the pope and the hierarchy to exalt themselves and to dominate.

9

In the Roman Church the administration of the sacraments, rather than the preaching of the word of God, is the main duty of the priest. Catholic apologists deduced a theological principle called the Incarnational principle or the law of Incarnation from the Incarnation of Christ by logical inference, and with the principle the Roman Church justifies its grandiose sacramental system. The Incarnation (Christ's taking a human body) is regarded as a foundation of the Catholic doctrines of the sacrament and of the church.

The above-mentioned theological principle would be valid, in our view, if it were understood in the limited sense that Christianity is sacramental in character because through the Incarnation of Christ "body and matter" have been shown to be capable of being the vehicle of God's grace and power. For example, the whole universe is sacramental of divine glory and power (Romans 1:20). For another example, the body of Jesus became a means of divine grace and miraculous healing (Mark 5:25-30).

To apply the principle beyond that, and to claim that the Church and its sacraments are a channel of transmitting spiritual gifts is a different matter. I maintain that to deduce such a theological principle from the Incarnation of Christ by logical inference and to legitimize with it the extreme ecclesiactical, sacramentalisitic religion as we see in the Roman Catholic Church is illegitimate. It has no sufficient basis in the New Testament. In the New Testament the Incarnation of Christ is primarily linked to his atoning death on the cross, and only indirectly to the church and its sacraments. In the first letter of Peter we read, "He (Christ) himself bore our sins *in his body* on the cross; by his wounds you were healed" (I Peter 2:24, emphasis added). On the cross the body of Christ became the means of God's redemption of mankind. The atoning death of Christ is more closely linked to the sacraments of the church than the Incarnation is. For the link between the death of Christ and the Lord's Supper (the eucharist) see I Corinthians 11:23-26. For the link between the death of Christ and baptism see Romans 6:3-4 and Colossians 2:11. Baptism, like the Lord's Supper, is a proclamation of Christ's death and resurrection and so is closely bound up with preaching. It is a dying to self and being reborn to a new life in

Christ. The going down into the waters symbolizes a burial and the coming up from the waters a resurrection.

In the New Testament centrality belongs to the cross rather than to the Incarnation. The Incarnation took place primarily for the sake of the event of the cross. So we read this in John's epistle:

> *This is love: not that we loved God, but that*
> *He loved us and sent His Son as an atoning*
> *sacrifice for our sins.*
>
> <I John 4:10>

Christ himself clearly stated for what purpose he took the human body and came to this world:

> *The Son of Man did not come to be served,*
> *but to serve, and to give His life a ransom for many.*
>
> <Matthew 20:28>

Thus the cross, rather than the Incarnation, is central. The apostle Paul calls the Christian gospel "the word of the cross" (I Corinthians 1:18) and says, "I determined to know nothing among you except Jesus Christ and him crucified." (I Corinthians 2:2). In the fourth gospel, John, the author, refers to the Incarnation merely in one verse (1:14), but he devotes two long chapters (18 and 19) to describe and expound Christ's suffering and death on the cross. For Paul, as we noted earlier, reconciliation with God through Christ's death, the forgiveness of sin and what he terms "justification" are closely related concepts. These constitute the central theological thought of Paul. His teachings about the church and the sacraments are secondary.

In Roman Catholicism, however, the church and the sacrament hold a dominant place, making it an ecclesiastical saramentalist religion. In this religion the Roman church claims to have received from Christ the "fullness of the means of salvation" (*Catechism* No.830) and to be "the minister of redemption". But in the New

Testament the church is not so much "the minister of redemption" as the people of God to be redeemed.

10

There is an additional difficulty with the ecclesiastical, sacrmentalist religion of the Catholic Church. In the Roman Catholic Church, as I have already pointed out, the church, the sacrament and the priest come between God and man. As a result, the personal relationship of man to God is hindered. Inevitably Roman Catholicism has become a rather impersonal and impersonalizing religion. It is difficult to regard Roman Catholicism as a personalist religion despite its affirmation that God is a personal God. The God of the Roman Church is a personal God with qualifications. The Catholic idea of God is metaphysical and static, conceived in the categories of essence and being. The Catholic idea of God is metaphysical and static, conceived in the categories of essence and being whereas the biblical idea of God is personal and dynamic, and is conceived in the categories of will, freedom, action and love. Aristotelian ontology (a theory of being) entered into Catholic philosophy and theology decisively through Thomas Aquinas in the 13th century, and ever since it has exerted a great influence. Some biblical scholars and theologians regard it as a pagan philosophy and as an antithesis to the Christian thought. The notion opposite to that of a personal God (God as a Person) is that the ultimate reality is something like a mindless impersonal structure of the world or an impersonal cosmic law or a supra-personal Being. Between the two are varying positions. As "person" represents the highest dimension and as such there is no category adequate to define person with, it is impossible to give a definition. But to speak from our human experience, a person is an agent and a selfhood with an independent centre of consciousness, with a will and a capacity for fellowship with other persons. In the Old Testament God speaks of Himself as "I". Indeed, He used the word "I" when He revealed His name to Moses. (Exodus 6:2-3)

"The incarnational structure" of grace and salvation and the notion that the Church is the extension of the Incarnation of Christ are not plain teachings of the New Testament, but are assertions which were deduced by way of stretching the meaning of the word "flesh" in John 1:14. I hold this to be an interpretation out of the context.

Above I pointed out that what the Roman apologists call "the Incarnational principle", "the law of Incarnation" and "the Incarnational structure of grace and salvation" and the grandiose Catholic doctrines of the church and the sacraments were deduced by logical inference. There are more doctrines of this kind. The doctrine of the immaculate conception of Mary is another illustration. The Catholic doctrine about Mary was made by logical inference. The Roman Church is in the habit of appealing to "logical inference" when every other kind of evidence is wanting. Actually the Marian cult first arose among lay people early in the Middle Ages under pagan influence. This was partly due to the false teaching of the Roman Church which portrayed Christ as a severe merciless Judge. So people needed someone like a loving mother who would intercede for them. This popular demand led to the rise of the Marian cult and the demand was met by the cult. The cult produced deplorable abuses. With many Catholics the focus of their religion is, so it appears, Mary rather than God or Christ. The Roman Church would not officially approve this cult, but allows it without interference. This Marian cult is a serious perversion of the Gospel of Christ and a subversion of the Christianity of the New Testament.

To deduce a theological principle and religious doctrines by logical inference is a practice unknown in the Bible. The proclamations of Jesus and the New Testament as well as the Old Testament are conspicuous for the absence of such logical inference and abstract reasoning. The characteristics of the theology of the New Testament are that it attaches absolute significance and value to God's saving acts which took place in time and history and that it is a "personalist religion" through and through. The saving acts of God as historical events rather than logic are a matter of primary concern for the New Testament. The biblical scholar G. Ernest Wright rightly said, " ...the central message of the Bible is a proclamation of a Divine action ... The Biblical faith is first and foremost a confessional recital of the gracious and redemptive acts of God." (God Who Acts by G.E. Wright (1952). pp.120)

11

Then how are we to interpret the Lord's Supper? The New Testament has comparatively little to say about celebrating the Lord's Supper. In the apostolic times, the celebration of the Lord's Supper was regarded as an activity of the entire congregation (I Corinthians 10:16, 11:20). Its celebration was not the minister's exclusive privilege or duty while the congregation remained in passivity, looking on. Of course, for the sake of order and dignity of the celebration someone was needed to preside. If an apostle was present, probably he presided it (Acts 2:42, 20:7, 11). In the absence of an apostle, prophet or evangelist, this duty would naturally fall to one of the local presbyters or bishops. (The "bishop" in the apostolic times was not the same office as the monarchical bishop of the Catholic Church.)

A crucial question with regard to the understanding of the Lord's Supper is whether the supper is to be understood as a channel of spiritual gifts being really bestowed on the recipient or as a visible sign and symbol of God's invisible grace and as a memory of Christ's death. Those who believe in the real spiritual gifts given through the sacrament are called the sacramentalists. The Catholic Church takes this position.

I have discussed this question at the early part of this Appendix. According to the Catholic doctrine of the sacrament the sacramental grace "sanctifies" the recipient of the sacrament. In simple terms, the sacrament is held to make the recipient a morally better person. I regret to suggest, however, that there is no observable evidence that the sacraments of the Catholic Church really change the recipients and make them more loving and self-sacrificing persons. We are more interested in seeing the changed lives of people, their changed communities and changed country than hearing the abstract doctrinal theory of the Church. I have discussed this topic in Chapter 11.

We are seeking to find the concept of the sacrament which is true to the biblical teaching and consonant with the "personalist" understanding of Christianity which is, in our view, the true understanding.

The Catholic Church's doctrines about the eucharist, especially the doctrine of "Transubstantiation", contradict the teaching of the Scripture. The concept of the sacrament which is consonant with Christianity as a "personalist religion" is to conceive the sacrament as a visible sign and symbol of God's saving grace, rather than as means of channeling spiritual gifts for salvation (as in the Roman Church).

The Lord's Supper can also be understood as the visible counterpart of the gospel message proclaimed. The accounts in the Synoptic gospels suggest that the Lord's Passover was originally a family festival for the historical memory and commemoration of the saving acts of God at the Exodus (Exodus 12:1-28; 13:1-16). As a matter of fact, Jesus instituted the Lord's Supper at the Passover meal on the Passover night (Matthew 26:17-28; Mark 14:12-24; Luke 22:7-20). When instituting the Lord's Supper, Jesus said, "Do this in remembrance of me" (Luke 22:19; I Corinthians 12:24-25). Indeed the apostle Paul says that Christ "our Passover (lamb)" has been sacrificed (I Corinthians 5:7). Christ in his sacrificial death for men is described here as our Passover (lamb), which is a recollection of the ceremonial slaying of the lamb for use in the feast (Exodus 12:1-28). When John the Baptist saw Jesus, he said, "Behold, the Lamb of God that takes away the sins of the world" (John 1:29, 36). Peter too says, "You were redeemed … with the precious blood of Christ, a lamb without blemish or defect" (I Peter 1:18-19). Elsewhere in the New Testament as well, Christ is called the lamb" (Acts 8:32; Revelation 5:6, 7, 12). The atoning death of Christ for the redemption of human beings was the fulfillment of the Passover event which was one of the foreshadowings of God's final salvation through Christ. The Lord's Supper is for Christians the celebration in which they "remember" this saving event which occurred some 2000 years ago, just as the Passover feast was for the Israelites the celebration in which they "remembered" and commemorated God's saving event which took place during the Exodus (Exodus 12:14; Deuteronomy

16:3). As the old deliverance was followed by the covenant of Sinai, sealed by sacrificial blood, so the deliverance in Christ is linked with the new covenant promised in Jeremiah 31 (Hebrews 8:6-13). The Lord's Supper instituted at the Passover time was linked to the new covenant by the blood of Jesus (Luke 22:20; I Corinthians 11:23:26). In the Christian Church the Lord's Supper came to replace the old Passover meal. In conclusion, I would like to maintain that Christ's words "This is my body" are to be understood as meaning "This represents my body."

My presentation above reflects the view of the non-Catholic Churches. Although most non-Catholic Churches understand, so it seems, the Lord's Supper (Eucharist) as a memory of the atoning death of Christ, it is not a mere memorialism, but acknowledges a spiritual presence of Christ during the Supper. Did not our Lord promise that where two or three come together in his name, there he is in the midst of them (Matthew 18:20)?

12

We have already devoted much space for the discussion of the question of the sacrament and found that a "higher" view of the sacrament has no solid biblical basis. On the basis of the saying of Jesus recorded in John 6:63 which qualifies any allusion to the Lord's Supper in 6:51-58, some biblical scholars maintain that John the author of the fourth gospel is anti-sacramentalist. In John 6:63 Jesus said, "it is the Spirit who gives life; the flesh profits nothing; the words that I have spoken to you are spirit and are life." Also Peter says, "You have been born again not of seed which is perishable but imperishable, that is, through the living and abiding Word of God" (I Peter 1:23). In both passages, the point is that the rebirth and sanctification of a believer are through the Word of God with the Spirit of God working together. This teaching is clearly remote from the teaching of the Roman Church that a believer is reborn and sanctified through the sacramental grace. The phrase and idea of "sacramental grace" are not found in the New Testament. The impersonal concept of the grace of God is perfectly consistent with the impersonal nature of the religion of the Roman Catholic Church. In the New Testament, the grace of God is the loving-kindness, mercy, and undeserved favor of God, and to Paul it is the free, forgiving love of God. The grace of God is, in essence, a personal encounter or meeting between the believer and God, which can be described in terms of a personal relationship. In contrast, in the sacramentalist religion of the Catholic Church the grace of God is principally conceived as "sacramental grace". The sacramental grace is of a *quasi-material* nature which is "infused" into the soul of the believer through the channel of the sacraments consecrated by the priest of the church. It is something like a "medicine" which has power to heal the fallen nature due to sin. It works miraculously in the believer and transforms (sanctifies) him. it is an impersonal operation. Thus, even in the receiving of God's grace, the personal relation between the believer and God is missing. The whole religious life in the Roman Church has links with holy things sanctified by rituals. This impersonal nature of the sacramentalist priestly religion of the Catholic Church is perhaps the main reason for the amazing popularity of the Marian cult in the Roman Church. Human souls cannot be fully satisfied with impersonal sacramental religion. They hunger for a personal and intimate relation with the Divine. Catholics have found this in their devotion to the Virgin Mary.

I have discussed in the foregoing the impersonal character of the Catholic doctrines of grace and the church. Now I propose to consider one more doctrine of the Roman Church, the Catholic doctrine of faith. The three doctrines are linked. I will point out the impersonal character of the Catholic concept of faith, and will show that it is profoundly different from the biblical concept of faith.

In the ecclesio-centric religion of the Roman Catholic Church "faith" is primarily a mental assent to the doctrines of the church, which were formulated and imposed on the church members by the authoritative Church. The doctrines of the church are held to be supernatural saving truth which the church members must accept obediently "on the authority of the Church" which has received infallible teaching authority from Christ. In this Catholic concept of faith, a believer's personal relationship to God is missing or obscured.

I pointed out that there is a great discrepancy between the Catholic doctrine of faith and the biblical notion of faith which is to be characterized as "personalistic". I would like to state the crux of the issue. In the Scripture faith is not merely a belief in the doctrinal propositions about God, namely, that God as the Creator and Ruler of heaven and earth exists, that God's power and wisdom are infinite, and so forth, not to mention that faith as an assent to the doctrines of the church is worlds apart from the teaching of the Holy Scripture. The New Testament says that even the devils believe that there is one God and tremble (James 2:19).

Faith is more than a belief in doctrinal propositions; it is a personal trust in God's mercy and His faithfulness to the promise (word) He has made. I express the point another way. The primary object of faith is not a set of doctrines about God but God Himself. Faith itself is understood essentially in terms of personal relationship of man with God, which was initiated by God Himself Who is a personal God, and this initiation is a divine act of mercy and grace.

Above I emphasized that in the Scripture faith is primarily a personal trust in God's mercy and in His faithfulness to the promise (word) He has made. I give Romans 4:18-22 as an example to illustrate the point. In this passage the apostle Paul explains Abraham's unwavering faith in God's promise. Abraham was a hundred years old and his wife Sarah's womb was dead. Yet Abraham believed God's promise that Sarah would give birth to a son and that through the son he (Abraham) would become the father of nations. "Against all hope, Abraham in hope believed and so became the father of many nations, just as it had been said to him (by God)" (verse 18). "He (Abraham) did not waver through unbelief regarding the promise of God, but was strengthened in his faith and gave glory to God, being fully persuaded that God had power to do what he had promised. This is why it was credited to him as righteousness" (verses 20 to 22). Based on this Old Testament narrative about Abraham's faith and about his faith being credited to him as righteousness (Genesis

15:1-6), the apostle Paul formulated his central theological doctrine of "justification by faith through grace".

A deplorable phenomenon in the Catholic Church is that the place and role of the word of God have been obscured by giving primacy to the sacrament; as a result, an awakening aroused by the word of God in the individual believer's heart is not adequately understood. In other words, one of the most important characteristics of the biblical faith tends to be ignored. With the Holy Spirit working together with it, the word of God, written or preached, is heard by the believer as a personal call and address of God. As this is an inner event occurring in his heart, the external things such as the sacrament do not play a prominent role, and the relationship between the believer and God becomes a personal one as in the case of the patriarch Abraham (Genesis 12:1-4). In the personal dialogue with God, external things, meant to be of help, may become an impediment, diminishing the urgency and seriousness of God's call. Clearly in this situation the sacrament and even the church as an institution can play a hindering role.

That the New Testament ascribes primacy to the word of God rather than the sacrament is evident to those who read the New Testament closely. Jesus said, "Man shall not live on bread alone, but on every word that proceeds out of the mouth of God" (Matthew 4:4). Again, "It is the Spirit who gives life: the flesh profits nothing; the words that I have spoken to you are spirit and are life" (John 6:63). In the biblical faith the word of God and the working of the Holy Spirit are inseparable (Isaiah 59:21; Acts 10:44; Ephesians 6:17). Peter said to Jesus, "Lord, to whom shall we go? You have words of eternal life" (John 6:68). The apostles declared that their main duty was the ministry of the word of God, and not relief work or the administration of the sacraments (Acts 6:2, 10:48; I Corinthians 1:17). Peter, whom the Roman Church counts on as its main supporting pillar, actually contradicts the Catholic Church on a number of important issues.

The doctrine of the word of God is, in essence, the doctrine of God as a Person. This is obvious because only a person, divine or human, can speak words and communicate his mind to others.

Therefore it is quite natural that the faith of the New Testament which attributes primacy to the word of God is a personalist religion. But this personal character of the biblical faith does not refer merely to individual piety. The people of God as a whole have a corporate personality as we see in the writings of God's prophets. The designation of the church as the bride of Christ, of God as Father or Husband of His people shows this. See Isaiah 1:2-3, 63:16 for example. Needless to say, what I call the personalist faith should not be confused with individualistic or privatistic religion.

13

The "personalist" interpretation of Christianity is to be differentiated not only from the sacramentalistic interpretation but also from the legalistic interpretation of it. A personalist interpretation of Christianity articulates its understanding in personal terms like love, grace, trust, forgiveness and a personal relationship of man to the gracious God. What I call the "legalistic interpretation" refers to the Catholic doctrine of the church and the clerical hierarchy which are conceived in legal terms (such as authority, power, organization, administration, jurisdiction, order, obedience and submission). The religion conceived in legal terms inevitably becomes authoritarian and impersonal. Indeed the church with such an organizational juridical power structure emerged early in the Middle Ages, and it remains so until today. The sacramentalism, ecclesiasticism, legalism and authoritarianism of the Roman Church have had the decisive effect of "depersonalizing" the religion. I quote here the words of Charles Davis, a former Catholic theologian and priest, who questioned the credibility of the Catholic Church and left it, "For me Christian commitment is inseparable from concern for truth and people. I do not find either of these represented by the official Church. There is concern for authority at the expense of truth, and I am constantly saddened by instances of the damage done to persons by the working of an impersonal and unfree system. Further I do not think that the claim that the Church makes as an institution rests on any adequate biblical and historical basis. The Church in its existing form seems to me to be a pseudo-political structure from the past." (A Question of Conscience by Charles Davis, 1967, pp. 16) This is a valuable testimony of a former insider, of the Catholic Church.

In conclusion, I believe that the Roman Catholic Church, as the result of the ecclesiastic, sacramentalistic and the legalistic interpretation of Christianity and also as the result of a massive influx of pagan cults and practices into the Church over the course of its historical development, has transmutated into a partly pagan religion and only partly retains biblical faith. The renowned Catholic religious writer Friedrich Heiler presented an important proposition in his monumental work Der Katholizismus (1923) when he asserted that Roman Catholicism is a complex of seven different types of religion. It is a religion of primitive superstition; a legalistic religion; a rationalistic religion of theological doctrines; an esoteric mystery-religion; an evangelical religion of salvation; and a mystical religion. In my view, Heiler proposition is penetrating and insightful, and is largely true. This mutation of Christianity is to be explained partly at least by the fact that since early in the Middle Ages the pope and his curia did not have much respect for the Holy Scripture and in practice largely ignored it.

14

One last point. Jesus Christ had a great respect for the prophets of God in the Old Testament. According to the prophets, God demands justice and mercy in human relations and in the society rather than sacrifices, rituals and solemn assembly in the temple (Isaiah 1:10-17; Micah 6:6-8; Amos 5:21-24; Hosea 6:6). Obviously this fact has relevance in our appraisal of the ecclesiastical, sacramentalist (ritualist) religion of the Roman Church.

The conception of "worship" as the internal spiritual service of God was developed by the prophets and was even brought into opposition to the ritual service of sacrifice (Micah 6:6-8; Psalm

40:6). Christ stands in the prophetic tradition. Through the prophet Jeremiah, God said:

> The time is coming when I will make a new covenant with the house of Israel and with the house of Judah ... I will put my law in their minds and write it on their hearts.
>
> <31:31, 33>

This promise of the internalization and fulfillment of God's covenant was accomplished by Christ (Hebrews 8:8-13, 10:12-16). Christ gave primacy to the internal spiritual element.

> Our Lord Jesus said: "God is spirit. The true worshipers will worship the Father in spirit and truth, for they are the kind of worshipers the Father seeks." (John 4:23-24) This is the great and foremost commandment. *The second is like it, you shall love your neighbor as yourself. On these two commandments depend the whole Law and the Prophets.*
>
> <Matthew 22:37-40; John 17:26, 16:27>

> Closely related with this is that Christ showed little interest in ritual worship. He said, "God is Spirit; and those who worship Him must worship in spirit and truth"
>
> <John 4:24>

The development of the biblical faith from the Old Testament to the New was in the direction of internalization and personalization. But the Roman Church's ecclesiasticism (external, juridical, authoritarian, and institutional) and sacramental ritualism are oriented in a different direction, namely, on the externals of religion. This is essentially a different kind of religion.

But this internalization of the biblical religion should not be taken to mean that Christianity is merely a religion of personal piety. That is a dangerous misunderstanding. But Christianity is "big" enough as to have room for personal piety.

The true Christian faith is, I believe, a matter of the heart rather than external things like institution and habits of worship, performing the rituals as prescribed. Our Lord Jesus said "God is spirit. The true worshipers will worship the Father in spirit and truth, for they are the kind of worshipers the Father seeks."(John 4:23-24)

Although the writer uses the word "religion" in reference to Christianity in this book, he does not mean to say that Christianity is simply one religion among many others, nor even that it is the greatest among them. Christianity is the unique religion that has come from God.

XIII

THE POPE'S TREATIES WITH BRUTAL DICTATORS

IN 1933, AS I ALREADY noted, the Pope concluded a Concordat (treaty) with Hitler's Germany. Several years earlier (1929) the Vatican had signed a similar treaty called the Lateran Treaty with Benito Mussolini, the Fascist dictator of Italy. According to the terms of the Lateran Treaty, Roman Catholicism became the sole recognized religion in the country. Crucially, the Treaty acknowledged the right of the pope to impose within Italy the new Code of Canon Law. As I mentioned earlier, the Code of Canon Law is the body of internal law of the Catholic Church promulgated by the pope in 1917. It was designed to establish and maintain the pope's absolute power and unchallenged domination from the Roman centre over the Catholic Churches of the world.

Mussolini approved this Code of Canon Law. In return he demanded and received from the pope the guarantee that political action of the clergy and all those in religious orders would be prohibited and there would be no political and social Catholicism (article 43). Mussolini needed this to consolidate his absolute political dictatorship in Italy. This was virtually a mutual aid pact between Mussolini and the pope. It has been pointed out that there was affinity between this state dictatorship of Mussolini and the ecclesiastical dictatorship of the pope. The powerful democratic Catholic Popular Party which the Vatican had not supported and which was in many respects similar to the Catholic Centre Party in Germany was disbanded under mounting pressures, and its leader exiled.

Catholics were instructed by the Vatican to withdraw from politics as Catholics, leaving a political vacuum in which the Fascist regime was able to act freely. In the elections following the Lateran Treaty, priests throughout Italy were encouraged by the Vatican to support the Fascists, and the pope spoke of Mussolini as "a man sent by Providence".

Not surprisingly, Adolf Hitler, the future Nazi dictator praised the Lateran Treaty and hoped for an identical agreement for his future regime. A few days after the signing of the Lateran Treaty Hitler wrote an article for the newspaper Voelkisher Beobachter (People's Observer) on February 22, 1929 and said, "The fact that the Curia is now making its peace with Fascism shows that the Vatican trusts the new political realities far more than it did the former liberal democracy with which it could not come to terms". Turning to the German political situation, Hitler rebuked the (Catholic) Centre Party leadership for its stubborn attachment to democratic politics. "By truing to preach that democracy is still in the best interests of German politics, the Centre Party … is placing itself in stark contradiction to the spirit of the treaty signed today by the Holy See." Hitler also said, "The fact that the Catholic Church has come to an agreement with Fascist Italy … proves beyond doubt that the Fascist world of ideas is closer to Christianity than those of Jewish liberalism or even atheistic Marxism." As the Fascism of Mussolini and the Nazism of Hitler's Germany were similar ideologies, it was natural that the two dictators became allies during the Second World War. In 1933 the Vatican signed *the Reich Concordat* with Hitler's Germany, which was in practical purposes a mutual aid pact between the two dictators, namely the pope and Hitler, at the sacrifice of the well-being, integrity and honour of the Catholic Church in Germany. I will elaborate this point.

Hitler feared the resistance and opposition of political Christianity, whether Catholic or Protestant, to his National Socialism (Nazism), and was determined to find a way to neutralize the church, as far as its political influence was concerned. His fear came from his knowledge of the historical precedent of Catholic reaction to Bismarck's Kulturkampf (culture struggle). Otto von Bismarck (1815-98) was the first chancellor of the modern German Empire, and Kulturkampf refers to the conflict between the German imperial government and the Roman Catholic Church in the 1870s and 1880s chiefly over the control of educational and ecclesiastical appointments. Bismarck did not win in the bitter conflict. In a letter (1929) to a Catholic Nazi Father Magnus Goett, Hitler said, "I always and under all circumstances take it to be a misfortune when religion, regardless in which form, is joined to political parties." He also accused the Catholic Centre Party of waging a bitter conflict against the national idea since the end of the First World War.

As it happened, bolstered by the strength of the Catholic Centre Party, the Catholic Church in Germany saw an unprecedented growth and expansion, not only in religious but also in cultural and political terms. The Catholic population in Germany was about 23 million by 1930, about 35 percent of the nation. Catholic opposition to Hitler's National Socialism (Nazism) was strong and sustained in the press and from the pulpits. I give a few examples. In these accounts the writer is entirely indebted to John Cornwell's *Hitler's Pope* (1999). A Catholic Journalist Walter Dirks, writing in the August 1931 edition of the journal *Die Arbeit* (Labour), described the Catholic reaction to Nazism as "open warfare", and asserted that the ideology of Nazism "stood in blatant explicit contrast to the Church". In the spring of 1931, the Catholic Reichstag (Parliament) representative Karl Trossmann published a book entitled *Hitler and Rome* in which he described the National Socialists as a "brutal party that would do away with all the rights of the people." He said that Hitler was dragging Germany into a new war, a war that "would only end more disastrously than the last war." The Catholic author Alfons Wild also published a widely distributed essay entitled "Hitler and Catholicism" in which he declared that "Hitler's view of the world is not Christianity but the message of race, a message that does not proclaim peace and justice but rather violence and hate."

Meanwhile, two Catholic journalists, Frita Gerlich and Ingbert Naab, co-authored an article for the Munich-based journal Der Gerade Weg (The Straight Path), denouncing National Socialism. In the issue dated July 21, 1932 the writers said that "National Socialism means enmity with neighbouring countries, despotism in internal affairs, civil war and international war. National Socialism means lies, hatred, fratricide and unbounded misery. Adolf Hitler preaches the law of lies. You who have fallen victim to the deception of one obsessed with despotism, wake up!"

Thus, German Catholic journalists and writers accurately perceived the true nature of Hitler's Nazism and correctly predicted its consequences. Not only the journalists and writers, but average thinking Catholics also shared their view, according to Cornwell.

Likewise the Roman bishops also recognized the unchristian character of Nazism. The Catholic bishop's office in Mainz drew attention to the "Hitler Party's policy of racial hatred" and pointed out the fact that "the religious and educational policy of National Socialism is inconsistent with Catholic Christianity." Yet the Catholic bishops failed to produce a single unanimous document when they gathered for conference in the late autumn 1930. Instead, the president of the bishop's conference made a New Year statement, warning the Catholic Church in Germany against political extremism and the wickedness of racism.

In February 1931, the Bavarian bishops made a more specific directive for the clergy in their region. They said, "As guardians of the true teaching of faith and morals, the bishops must warn against National Socialism. So long and so far as it proclaims cultural and political options that are incompatible with Catholic teachings." The following month, the German Catholic archbishops stated in the clearest terms that National Socialism and Catholicism were incompatible, and repeated the key sentence of the Bavarian bishops' letter. Thus, there was a strong and united front of the Catholic Church in Germany against Hitler's National Socialism in 1931.

Then, how is it that Catholic antagonism to Nazism failed to materialize in the form of the confrontation Hitler greatly feared? The answer is that the Vatican intervened with superior authority to override the opposition of the German Catholic Church to Nazism. Why did the Vatican do that? Because the Vatican shrewdly perceived that having a concordat with Hitler's regime was in the best interest of reinforcing and keeping secure the pope's absolute centrist domination of the Catholic Church in Germany and elsewhere. All other considerations were secondary. The pope's lust for power and callous egotism were the main motive.

This is not the first time that the Vatican betrayed the high cause it is supposed to stand for. We have seen it in the Vatican's Lateran Treaty with the Fascist dictator Mussolini of Italy in 1929 as well. The Catholic historian Cornwell said, "The Holy See for centuries had been in the habit of signing treaties with monarchs and governments inimical to its beliefs and values." One will get a moral shock or one may not believe it. But there are almost innumerable cases of the "Holy" See's very unholy behavior in church history. Here I quote again the noteworthy remark of the Catholic Archbishop Luigi Puecher-Passavalli of Italy, "The personnel of the Pontifical Curia have produced in me an unconquerable conviction that never, never to the very end of the world, will they consent to renounce Temporal Power ... They will utilize every means (at one time public at another secret, at one time more violent at another less so) to repossess themselves of the Power at any and every price. Not Religion, not Piety, not Christianity, not Theology is the proper interest of the members of the Pontifical Curia, but the political advantage of political institution." This remark is, in our view, true not only of the members of the Pontifical Curia but also of the pope himself. This Italian archbishop had a long acquaintance with the Pope.

XIV

THE POPE'S CALLOUS EGOTISM

THE POPE'S CALLOUS EGOTISM WAS already shown, for instance, in its preoccupation with preserving Rome safe from the Allied bombing during the Second World War although there were other urgent matters which called for the Vatican's immediate attention and action. This was so much the case that it drew a British diplomat's sharp rebuke.

In the early 1930s the German Catholic Church, with its 23 million faithfuls, was a powerful independent constituency, together with the Catholic hierarchy and the Catholic Centre Party. The German Chancellor Hitler feared the opposition from the Roman Church united as a political force. As Hitler did not want to provoke a new *Kulturkampf* with the Catholic Church he avoided directly taking on the bishops. But something had to be done to neutralize them, and here the Vatican came to Hitler's aid, with its own ambitious project and goals. But as the pope Pius XI was in poor health, it was the Cardinal Secretary of State Eugenio Pacelli who conducted in the name of the pope the successful negotiation of the Reich Concordat with Hitler. This is the reason why Pacelli who took the papal office after Pius XI's death came to be called "Hitler's Pope" by Cornwell.

The basic requirement of the treaty from Hitler's point of view was the voluntary withdrawal of the clergy from the political and social action and the disbanding of the Catholic Centre Party in exchange for guaranteeing the religious rights of the Catholics. But before its disbanding the Party had to give legal force to the passing of the Enabling Act in the Reichstag (Parliament) that would grant Hitler the constitutional powers of dictatorship. When these requirements from Hitler were made known, the Catholic bishops vehemently rejected them. By 1933 in which the Concordat with Hitler's regime was signed and ratified, the brutal and despotic nature of the regime, its unChrichtian ideology and hatred, anti-Semitism and paganism were already apparent for all to see. This is why the German Catholic Church strongly opposed the Concordat with the Nazi regime.

To make a long story short, both the German Catholic bishops and the Centre Party capitulated to the will of the Vatican. Under the increasing pressure of the Vatican the bishops revoked their opposition to Hitler's National Socialism and endorsed the Concordat. The Catholic Centre Party also was compelled to support the Enabling Act at the critical parliamentary vote, and a few months afterwards disbanded. Thus the sole surviving democratic party worth the name in Germany disappeared.

Thus, Hitler got everything he demanded. The treaty called "the Reich Concordat" was formally signed in the Vatican on July 20, 1933. For its part, the Vatican too obtained what it valued most highly and desired most, the right to impose the Code of Canon Law on the Catholic Church in Germany. Article 31 on the Concordat acknowledged the Holy See's right to control and coerce the Catholic clergy in Germany with efficient sanctions through the Canon Law. Thus, the two dictators, the one political and the other ecclesiastical, got what they wanted at the expense of the integrity, honour and wellbeing of the German Catholic Church. There was a remarkable similarity between this authoritarian state of Hitler and the authoritarian church of the pope. During the negotiations with Hitler for the treaty the Vatican ignored the protests, demands and hopes of the German bishops and clergy. The Vatican's main concern was to reinforce the already formidable central power of the pope at the expense of all other matters. The Concordat was a triumph for canon law and a victory for the papacy. Cornwell made this comment regarding the Concordat, " ...A bid for unprecedented papal power ... had drawn the Catholic Church into complicity with the darkest forces of the era." This complicity helped Hitler. Along with other factors, it emboldened Hitler to make an adventure of starting a war which led to the Second World War. Thus the Vatican made some contribution to the outbreak of the War. There is no evidence that the Vatican prudently considered the consequences of the Concordat with Hitler. Its greatest concern was with advancing the pope's absolute power exercised from the Roman centre, including the pope's exclusive right to nominate the bishops of his choice. Human rights and social ethics were not matters of concern to the Vatican. Here we recall a remarkable statement noted earlier made by Cardinal Eugene Tisserant, "I fear that history will reproach the Holy See for having practiced a policy of selfish convenience and little else."

Cornwell plausibly argues that if there had been no Concordat with Hitler's regime, the German Catholic Church which was powerful and united against Hitler's National Socialism would have protested, refused to cooperate and resisted Hitler's policy, and history might have been different. Cornwell gives an account of a number of significant and even successful resistances and demonstrations before the Concordat, which compelled the Nazi authorities to retreat. "Had these protests been repeated and extended in a multiplicity of local instances across Germany, from 1933 onwards, the history of the Nazi regime might have taken a different course." The Holocaust might not have taken place, and the outbreak of the War might have been put off or even avoided. Then the history of Europe and of the world would have been very different.

After the Concordat, however, there were no more protests, demonstrations, or resistance. The German Catholic Church was demoralized and paralyzed under the tight control by the Vatican and the Nazi regime. The Church was sacrificed for the sake of establishing the centrist papal power.

The collapse of the once great Centre Party drove Catholics in ever greater numbers into the bosom of National Socialism. In other words they became Nazis themselves. The conversion of Catholics to the National Socialists, at first a trickle, now became "a great river", in the words of Cornwell. The current pope Benedict XVI too (who was crowned in April, 2005 after the death of the Pope John Paul II) joined as a youth the Hitler's youth organization (Hitler Jugend) in 1941. In domestic politics, the Reich Concordat integrated the Catholics and their bishops into the Nazi system. In foreign politics, it bestowed on the Nazi dictator the first international recognition.

Here I will examine the actions of the Vatican during the years of the World War II and in the years preceding and following the war, and also on the behaviour of the successors of Pope John XXIII after the Second Vatican Council. I take this focus because I think that their actions and behaviours reveal the real nature of the papacy and what the Roman popes seek after most. This will, in turn, throw light on the Roman Church and give us some insight into the religion with the name of Roman Catholicism. The account which follows is based on John Cornwell's historical work. *Hitler's Pope-the Secret History of Puis XII (1999)*. Cornwell was Senior Research Fellow at Jesus College, Cambridge, England; he is now in the department of history and philosophy of science at Cambridge University. He is an award-winning journalist and author. He authored three highly regarded books, two of which are on popes. He has written on Catholic issues for many publications around the world. His *Hitler's Pope* was an acclaimed best seller on the *New York Times*. Cornwell appears to be a Roman Catholic. *Hitler's Pope* is the previously untold story of Eugenio Pacelli, pope Pius XII (1939-58), who was arguably the most powerful and dangerous pope in modern history. Cornwell wrote *Hitler's Pope* drawing on research from secret Vatican and Jesuit archives made available to him.

The main point of Cornwell's thesis in this book is that the Vatican prompted events in the 1920s and 30s which helped Adolf Hitler's rise to power unopposed. It reveals the Vatican's egoistic ambitions to advance the pope's autocratic power over the entire Catholic Church, and thereby unintentionally contributed to the outbreak of the World War II. The Vatican struck a Concord with Hitler which gave him the first international recognition and also helped him move swiftly to a legal dictatorship while neutralizing the potential of Germany's 23 million Catholics (34 million after the Anschluss with Austria) to protest and resist. Not only that, but according to Cornwell, much earlier the Vatican was also responsible for a treaty with Serbia which contributed to the rising tensions that led to the World War I. Thus the Vatican's main concern was with advancing the papal power over the Roman Church not only in Germany but throughout the world, regardless of its consequences for world peace, the well-being of peoples, and the interests of the German Catholic Church which was the most powerful in the world. What is apparent is the lust for power and "callous egotism" of the pope.

Hitler's Pope gives a portrait of pope Pius XII, who took office in 1939 on the eve of the Second World War and remained in office until his death in 1958, as a narcissistic, power hungry manipulator who was prepared to lie, appease and collaborate with the Nazi dictator in order to accomplish his ecclesiastical program, all to protect and reinforce the absolute power of the papacy. *The Washington Post*, in its book review, said that Hitler's Pope "redefines the entire history of the 20th century." *The New York Times* Book Review also said, "Explosive ... (Cornwell) makes a case in Hitler's Pope that is very difficult to refute." Cornwell's account is difficult to refute because it is well-documented.

The pope's egotism was also revealed in the fact that throughout the war years Pius XII was obsessed with one issue above all others, namely the preservation of Rome from aerial bombardment by the Allied air forces. He feared that Allied bombers would destroy Rome and the Vatican as they did other cities in Europe. So he repeatedly requested that Rome be exempted and his efforts paid off. Critics pointed out that the pope was guilty of a double standard, and thought that he was perhaps afraid of being bombed in the Vatican.

Critics also pointed out that while being obsessed with the safety of Rome and the Vatican and making ceaseless attempts to protect Rome from the Allied bombing, the pope did practically nothing about the Holocaust (mass murders of Jews by the Nazis), or about the Catholic Croatians' campaign of terror and extermination against two million Serb Orthodox Christians (an act of "ethnic cleansing" before the term came into vogue) during the war years. The Croatian Catholics massacred one fourth of the two million Serbs between 1941 and 1945. Unlike the Nazi atrocities the Croatian atrocities are not widely known.

Regarding the pope's preoccupation with preventing the bombing of Rome, Francis D' Arcy Osborne, the British minister at the Holy See, resident in the Vatican at the time, confided in his diary on December 13, 1942. "The more I think of it, the more I am revolted by Hitler's massacre of the Jewish race on the one hand, and, on the other, the Vatican's apparently exclusive preoccupation with the … possibilities of the bombardment of Rome." A few days later, he wrote to the Cardinal Secretary of State (of the Vatican) that the Vatican "instead of thinking of nothing but the bombing of Rome should consider their duties in respect of the unprecedented crime against humanity of Hitler's campaign of extermination of Jews. "Osborne's diary was quoted by Owen Chadwick, in *Britain and the Vatican during the Second World War* (Cambridge, 1989). Throughout the period, urgent pleas had been coming to the Vatican for help from Jewish communities and organizations of the world. Osborne being the British minister of the Holy See was the main channel through whom the pope conducted the negotiation with Allies about preserving Rome from the aerial bombardment. The secretary of State of the Vatican is the second in rank and power to the pope. The Vatican, including the pope, was taught a moral lesson by a British diplomat. This is a shame of maximum magnitude for the Vatican, especially for the pope who claims to be the Vicar of Christ and the infallible teacher of faith and morals.

XV

THE SECOND VATICAN COUNCIL AND THE STALLED REFORM OF THE CATHOLIC CHURCH

WE HAVE SEEN THAT AFTER a long historical process the Popes' sole rule of the Catholic Church, rigidly centralized, bureaucratized and clericalized, was finally established, and continued to exist until the middle of the 20th century.

Then something unexpected happened. Pope John XXIII (1958-63), the son of an Italian peasant farmer, called the Second Vatican Council in 1959 with a view to pastoral renewal and the promotion of Christian unity. The pope attributed the calling of the historic council to a sudden inspiration of the Holy Spirit. He proclaimed the principle of "aggiornamento," that the Church should develop and change with society and history. He brought winds of change to the Vatican and the Roman Church, relaxing the stiffness of the centralized hierarchical power structure. This was an unprecedented, sudden development in the history of the papacy and of the Roman Catholic Church. So a large segment of Catholics within the Church hailed it with excitement, and the whole Christian world watched the development in surprise and high expectation.

The Council (1962-1965) made many decisions that gave rise to historic changes – in liturgy and biblical studies, dialogue with the Protestant and Orthodox Churches, and a declaration on religious freedom. But the single most important decision for change was the call for "collegiality", a code word for more democracy in the Roman Church and power sharing between the pope and the bishops. This was to put an end to the one-man rule of the Catholic Church of the world, to decentralize and deabsolutize the papacy and to end the ideology of papal power which was brought in by the First Vatican Council (1869-1870) and pursued ever since. Also the Council restored the biblical concept of the church as the people of God and placed it in tension with the organizational and juridical concept which has been the dominant concept in the Roman Church.

Not surprisingly, there was die-hard resistance and objection to the church reform from the traditionalists during and after the Council. Then very regrettably, John XXIII died during the Council before the decisions of the Council were implemented and the reform was entrenched. After John's death his successors, Paul VI and John Paul II, the curia and other traditionalist forces quickly overpowered the reform advocates, and returned the Roman Church to its old state. Their main objection was to "collegiality", and so the Roman Catholic Church headed back toward the old days. The new popes disagreed with their predecessor John XXIII on the issue of collegiality and totally ignored him. Many Catholics are perhaps unaware that there was a gigantic struggle in the Church over the reform of the Church and that the struggle is still on-going in some ways.

Among the major historic decisions made by the Council was the decision to set up the "Synod of Bishops". The Synod was meant to be the chief structural means of change. However, the papacy has been and still is the greatest obstacle to change and to the union of the Christian churches. Pope Paul VI himself has several times admitted that the papacy, under the present aspect, is a major obstacle to the union of the Churches.

Apparently here is a self-contradiction of the Roman Church. However, the Catholic Church has managed to avoid the self-contradiction by the usual claim that only the Roman Catholic Church headed by the pope who is the successor of Peter and the Vicar of Christ on earth is "the Church." We feel that this is an arrogance and pretension on the part of the Catholic Church. The arrogance appears even more remarkable when we consider the magnitude of corruption and deceit of this official Catholic Church as manifested in the successive employment of "forgeries"; "it has followed the Machiavellian practice of other kingdoms, condoning torture and assassination" (Garry Wills); sales of Indulgences, of ecclesiastical offices, and of God's grace and blessing in the Middle Ages. Renaissance popes who, while imposing celibacy on the priests with an iron hand, "lived in monstrous luxury, unbridled sensuality and uninhibited vice" (Hans Kueng); popes' seemingly insatiable lust for power; unceasing power struggles within and without the church; maneuvers; manipulative interpretations of the Bible to aggrandize the Roman Church and to exalt and empower the priestly caste; often being an enemy of the human rights, freedom and social justice; a papal tribunal called the Inquisition which existed for five centuries in Europe and burned alive to death many thousands of "heretics" and witches; the so-called crusades that slaughtered hundreds of thousands of Christians for not submitting to the papal authority and the papal church; seeking and establishing the autocratic power structure of the papacy at the expense of justice and humanity, of the peace of the world, of the wellbeing of people, and of the integrity and well-being of regional churches; the signing of treaties with brutal dictators for questionable mutual benefit; the would-be Vicar of Christ that kept silence in the face of the Nazi Holocaust of six million Jews, and his successors who disregard it and even defend him; the use of the name of Christ and religion to advance the interests of the papacy; and so on and on.

These historical facts indicate an astonishing moral and spiritual degeneration. It is unbelievable that the living Vicar of Christ and the Church founded by Christ and allegedly having been supernaturally protected by God went down to such a low state. The Roman Church itself has been the greatest victim of the popes' love of power across many centuries. The Roman Catholic Church is comparable to a large passenger ship that has been seized by a band of pirate on the high sea and has been forced to proceed in an altered wrong direction. We have used this analogy earlier.

XVI

THE POPE'S CLAIM TO THE PRIMACY

THE ROMAN CATHOLIC CHURCH CLAIMS that it was founded by Christ and is endowed with authority which is not less than divine. Unlike the church in the New Testament which is conceived primarily as the people of God, this authoritarian church has an ecclesiastical government run by the clerical hierarchy. The pope who is at the top of this hierarchy is held to have been divinely appointed, and he delegates authority to lower ranks of the clergy. So every parish priest shares in the authority of the Church, limited in its exercise by higher ranks of the hierarchy. It is claimed that "the Roman Pontiff has full and supreme jurisdiction over the universal Church," and submission to the Church headed by the pope is demanded of every Catholic. Catholics are also required to believe what is taught "on the authority of the Church". This dual demand, perhaps more than anything else, clearly reveals the authoritarian character of the Roman Catholic Church. It also shows unmistakably, in our view, the contrast between the two concepts of the church, namely, the Catholic and the biblical concept.

The pope's claim to authority which is no less than divine is chiefly based on a peculiar interpretation of Christ's saying to Peter recorded in Matthew 16:18-9. Christ said: *I say to you that you are Peter, and upon this rock I will build my church; and the gates of Hades shall not overcome it. I will give you the keys of heaven; and whatever you shall bind on earth will be bound in heaven, and whatever you shall loose on earth will be loosed in heaven.*

On these words the Roman Church bases its threefold claim that to Peter was given the first place among the apostles and indeed authority over them; that to Peter was given the power to forgive sin or to retain it, and so to open or close the gates of heaven to other men; and that to Peter was also given the power to transmit these powers to the man he is pleased to appoint as his successor. It is further claimed that the bishop of Rome, namely the pope, is the successor of Peter; therefore whatever powers were given to Peter have been passed on to the pope. The pope is in principle able to choose his successor if he wills, but under the current system, a new pope is elected by the College of Cardinals. The dogma of papal infallibility is also based on inference from the same words of Jesus in Matthew 16:18-19. This text has been invoked to claim the supremacy of the bishop of Rome (the pope) over all other bishops and over the Christian churches throughout the world.

It is intriguing to see how the above-mentioned stupendous claims are deduced from Matthew 16:18-19. It is by an unusual imagination and ingenious inference. It will be difficult or even impossible for an ordinary person to read in Matthew 16:18-19 what the Roman Church reads into it. The text does not plainly say those things the pope of Rome claims; certainly there is nothing in the text which refers to the Roman Church or the bishop of Rome.

The pope's claim was ignored until the 5th century even in the West, let alone in the East. Gradually, however, the papal claim to primacy came to be generally recognized in the West, if not in the East. Papal primacy was afterwards interpreted as the supremacy of the pope, and the pope claimed to be "the vicar of Christ" on earth. In *The Catechism of the Catholic Church*, we read:

For the Roman Pontiff, by reason of his office as Vicar of Christ ... has full, supreme, and universal power over the whole Church, a power which he can always exercise unhindered.

<No. 9882>

But the Catholic interpretation of Matt. 16:18-19 and the papal claims have serious difficulties. There is no biblical and historical evidence that the apostle Peter claimed such powers for himself or exercised them. There is rather contrary evidence. This means that the pope of Rome makes claim to powers which Peter himself did not make. Neither in the two epistles of Peter nor in the writings of the Church Fathers of the second and the third century is there a reference along the line that Peter claimed and actually exercised a special power beyond the commonly shared power of the apostles.

As Matthew 16:18-19 does not say in plain words that Jesus invested Peter with the above-mentioned threefold power and infallibility, it is apparent that the Roman Church obtained its interpretation by means of stretching the meaning of the text. Here we present the thesis that if one stretches the meaning of a biblical text in the manner the Catholic Church does, he can prove by the Bible almost any strange idea he happens to like. Such a method will distort the meaning of the biblical text. I remind the reader that I am not saying that the monarchical papacy of the Roman Catholic Church developed and was established based on its interpretation of Matthew 16:18-9 (and a few other biblical texts). This is not the case. The monarchical papacy was first established through the determined effort and struggles of the ambitious bishops of Rome, under the influence of the legalistic spirit of the ancient Romans and after the model of the Roman Empire. The papalist interpretation of the biblical texts and the elaborate argument were formulated by theologians many centuries later to provide a biblical and theological basis for what already existed, and to solidify it. The pope and the curia in the Middle Ages had no due respect for, nor practical concern with, the Holy Scripture and theology.

The Orthodox Church and the Anglican Church as well as the Protestant Churches do not accept the papalist interpretation of

Matthew 16:18, and they reject the dogma of papal primacy. They hold that the Roman interpretation is unjustified and the papal claim is unfounded. They also point out that the papal claim to primacy is the major reason that the Church of Jesus Christ remains divided despite the earnest plea of the Lord Jesus for unity (John 17:11, 21-22; 10:16). To this, Catholic theologians loyal to the pope invoke another dogma of the Roman Church, namely, the dogma of the Church's teaching authority (the so-called magisterium), and argue roughly as follows: The Catholic Church is the depository of the supernatural salvific truth of God. The Catholic Church alone, specifically the pope alone, has received the authority of infallibly interpreting and teaching the Bible. Therefore the non-Catholic Churches have no right to put forward an interpretation of the Bible which differs from what the Roman Church proclaims to be the true one.

Here an inevitable question is: On what ground does the teaching authority of the Catholic Church assert that it is divinely invested with the authority of infallibly interpreting the Bible, in the present case, Matthew 16:18? To answer this question it is claimed that the Roman Church's infallible teaching authority is justified by Matthew 16:18, and it is this very authority which infallibly interprets Matthew 16:18.

This is a typical circular argument. If there is a logic in this argument at all, it is good only within the closed circle. Outside the circle, it loses force and proves nothing. The closed circle also refers to the huge edifice of Roman Catholicism. Matt. 16:18, thus interpreted, is one of the major pillars supporting the grand edifice of the Roman Church.

Peter's eminence among the apostles is admitted. but Peter was eminent in a representative way, rather than in a leadership capacity. We can offer biblical evidence which, in our view, refute the papalist assertion of Peter's primacy.

a.   The leading position was seemingly held by James, the brother of our Lord, in the early years of the Church. Consider the Council at Jerusalem which is recorded in the fifteenth chapter of Acts, especially verses 13 to 29.

b. Regardless of who was the leader, the Council's decision was not one leader's authoritative action. The decision and its implementation were the Council's collegial action. What we see here is the "collegiality" of the apostles rather than the sole dictatorship like the monarchical papacy of the Roman Church.

c. The apostles as a body in Jerusalem sent Peter and John to Samaria on a mission (Acts: 14-17).

d. Paul withstood Peter to the face in the presence of others when he found Peter's action to be against the principle of the Gospel (Galatians 2:1-14).

e. There was a rough division of the mission field among the apostles. Peter was the apostle to the Jews while Paul was to the Gentiles (Galatians 2:6-9). Peter was not an overall supervisor.

f. The circumcised believers (Jewish Christians) criticized Peter for the latter's having eaten with the Gentile Christians (Acts 11:1-3).

I would like to elaborate on a, b, c and d. In the days of the apostles, it appears that the prominent leader was James, the brother of Jesus, rather than Peter. The story in Acts 15 about the historic Council of the apostles and the elders who gathered to discuss a vitally important theological issue shows this. In the meeting of the Council Peter made an important contribution, but it was James who made the final conclusive speech and his proposal was adopted as a whole and implemented. It appears that James acted as the chairman at the Council. Elsewhere the apostle Paul says that James, Peter and John were "reputed to be pillars" of the Jerusalem church (Galatians 2:9). Paul also gives an interesting account about a significant incident. He says that he rebuked Peter in the presence of people for Peter's hypocrisy and wrong action (Galatians 2:1). If Peter were recognized as the supreme leader set apart by Christ from other apostles as the Roman Church asserts, it is improbable that Paul would dare to rebuke Peter in the presence of people.

Furthermore, the way Peter acted in the incident is not that of an undisputed leader.

Acts 8:14 says, "Now when the apostles in Jerusalem heard that Samaria had received the word of God, they sent there Peter and John, who came down and prayed for them, that they might receive the Holy Spirit." Obviously the apostles in Jerusalem consulted on the matter and acted as a body, and sent Peter and John on a mission. Here there is no indication that Peter was recognized by the apostles as the undisputed leader invested with special authority and status by Christ as Rome asserts. There are a few more biblical passages which seem to indicate that it was James, rather than Peter, who was regarded as the leading personality (Acts 21:18, 12:17). In the two epistles attributed to Peter, Peter does not say anything which suggests his special position and authority. Rather he speaks as one of many (elders). Also in neither of the two epistles does the word "church" appears. Time and again Peter mentions the prophets of God with high respect; this line of thought is not congruous with the ecclesiastic sacerdotal religion which Roman Catholicism is. Further, sadly for the Roman Church, Peter taught the doctrine of the priesthood of all believers (I Peter 2:9). This doctrine undermines any priestly institution set up in the Christian Church.

Who is Peter? Peter is asserted to be the head of the apostolic college; and the pope of Rome claims to be Peter's successor. Based on Jesus' saying to Peter, "The gates of hell shall not overcome the church," it is claimed that the Church of Rome is under the supernatural protection of God. Thus the prestige of the Roman Church is greatly increased. But Peter said things which would damage the claimed prestige and authority of the Church. For example, Peter said:

> For it is time for the judgement (of God) to begin with the house of God; if it begins with us first, what will be the outcome for those who do not obey the gospel of God? (1 Peter 4:17) "The house of God" refers to the church.

The apostles and the early church believed that Christ's second coming in glory and God's judgment of the world were impending. They did not expect that there would be a long period of the Church on earth that would last for thousands years. Peter warned that God's judgment would "begin with the house of God". This warning contradicts the pretentious claims of the Roman Church that as the Mystical Body of Christ and the extended and continued Incarnation of Christ, the Catholic Church is vested with the authority which is not less than divine, and is infallible and incorruptible, and that the Roman Church is the Kingdom of God on earth and as such is free from the relativity and ambiguity of history. It is a common teaching of the Old and the New Testament that God will judge His own people first (Jeremiah 7:12-15, 25:29; Ezekiel 9:6; Amos 3:2; Isaiah 10:12; I Peter 4:17). In the New Testament the church is primarily the people of God, called to modesty and lowliness. Peter thinks of the church as the people of God (2:9-10). The people of God are those who have been chosen and called by God and who are now pilgrims and exiles in the world (1:1-3, 2:11). For Peter, the church is the flock of God (5:2) and Christ is the Chief Shepherd (5:4). Peter says that the ministers of the church are shepherds of the sheep. Jesus himself called his followers the "little flock" (Luke 12:32) of which he was the Shepherd. He said that there were "other sheep" besides and he will bring them so that they become one flock with one Shepherd (John 10:16). The image of the church as sheep is anything but self-exalting and authoritarian. It is also worth noting that the church is differentiated from the ministers of the church in the Acts of the Apostles (15:4, 22, 14:23 and 20:28). The essential component of the church is the people, rather than the clergy.

To sum up, for Peter the church is the chosen people, pilgrims in the world and the flock of God. The humble and lowly image of the church of God which is conveyed here is just the contrary of the grandiose triumpalistic image of the church as conceived by the Roman Catholic Church. Yet the pope of Rome claims that he is the successor of Peter. In the New Testament there is another figure of speech about the church, namely, that the church is the bride of

Christ. To think of the humble people of God who call on the name of the Lord Jesus Christ, as "the bride of Christ" makes sense. To think of the authoritarian self-exalting hierarchical church as the bride of Christ is contrary to the New Testament depiction. We continue our study of the words Jesus said to Peter as recorded in Matthew's gospel:

> I will give you the keys of the kingdom of heaven; whatever you bind on earth will be bound in heaven, and whatever you loose on earth will be loosed in heaven.
>
> <Matthew 16:19>

How are these words to be interpreted? If they are interpreted literally, such an interpretation creates enormous difficulty. It is to be borne in mind that Jesus used many parables, metaphors and symbolical words in his teaching.

Consider another saying of Jesus to Peter which is recorded in the same chapter of Matthew.

> "Out of my sight, Satan! You are a stumbling block to me, you do not have in mind the things of God, but the things of men."
>
> <Matthew 16:23>

Jesus said this when Peter rebuked him for having foretold that he (Jesus) would suffer in Jerusalem and be killed. If this saying is taken literally, Peter is now "Satan", the devil. We notice that Jesus said exactly the same thing to the devil when the latter tempted Jesus to worship him (Matthew 4:8-10). "Out of my sight, Satan", said Jesus. There is nothing strange in Jesus calling the evil tempter "Satan", but to call Peter his disciple "Satan" is another matter. Is it conceivable that Jesus builds his Church on "Satan" and gives him the keys of the kingdom of heaven? The literal interpretation of Jesus' saying to Peter creates great difficulty. If we understand these words as symbolical or figurative sayings, the difficulty will be lessened greatly. One may interpret that when Jesus said these harsh words to

Peter, he (Jesus) was addressing whatever in Peter has been perversely influenced by the prince of evil. Then Peter is not literally Satan. The Catholic doctrines of the church, the sacrament and the papacy were formulated by way of literal interpretation of a few biblical passages and also by arbitrary stretching of the meaning of the words.

"Binding" and "loosing" were idiomatic expressions in rabbinical Judaism to indicate the proclamation of rulings either forbidding or permitting various kinds of activity. The words "binding" and "loosing" are not to be taken literally.

There is another noteworthy problem. It is the fact that this saying of Christ recorded in Matthew 16:18-19 is not found in the gospels of Mark, Luke and John, but in Matthew only. Not only so with the exception of Matthew 16:18 and Matthew 18:17, the word "church" does not appear in the gospels. This surprising fact calls for an explanation. The fact that the parallel passage is missing in Mark's gospel and that Mark does not make a single reference to the church is remarkable. It is remarkable especially because Mark was a close associate of the apostle Peter, so close that Peter called Mark "my son" (I Peter 5:13). Mark's gospel is believed to depend mainly on the sources that derived from Peter.

Even if we allow that Matthew 16:18-19 is an authentic saying of Christ, that Peter was given primacy and authority over the other apostles and that Peter alone received the keys of heaven as the Roman Church asserts, it does not follow that the Roman pope's claim to primacy as Peter's successor is legitimate. For there is a crucial point to consider. The papal claim stands or falls with the truth or otherwise of the assertions that whatever were the powers given to Peter, he was empowered to transmit them to his successor, and that the bishop of Rome, among a number of bishops, became Peter's sole successor. Regarding the transmission of Peter's office and power to the bishop of Rome (later the pope), a Scottish theologian made a decades-long investigation and wrote, "For this assertion there is nothing that can be called evidence" (C. Anderson Scott: Romanism and the Gospel (1937), p. 188). Many other theologians and church historians have reached the same conclusion. We could say that there is a consensus about this question among reliable scholars. Only some loyal Catholic scholars disagree. We suspect that even some of the Catholic scholars, if they are good scholars, waver in their minds. However, the fact is that no scholars, whether Catholic or not, has produced so far any solid historical or biblical evidence to support the papal claim to primacy.

There have been numerous forged documents to legitimize the monarchical papacy and its power. But their being forgeries was later detected by historians. For example, a second-century forgery which gives the earliest list of the bishops of Rome is a papalist attempt to produce a false evidence of Peter's episcopate in Rome. The attempt failed because historians have uncovered that it was a forgery. As we have already noted, forged documents appeared again and again in the history of the Roman Church, mostly to reinforce the papal power. The papal curia used these forgeries and they were quite effective in attaining its objective. We think that if the popes had not used these forgeries, the Roman papacy would be different from what it is today. Also it is to be pointed out that some of the old forgeries are still being used in unnoticeable ways. Theologians have noted them specifically. We have already dealt with this question. Yet the Vatican does not appear to be embarrassed by this and simply ignores it. This is a bizarre, incredible phenomenon. Do they have a right conscience? This writer finds it hard to expel the impression that "truth" is a scarce commodity in the catalogue of the claims and announcements made by the popes of Rome since the Middle Ages. The Catechism of the Catholic Church which was approved and ordered to be published by the pope John Paul II in 1992 gave the definition of sin as follows, "Sin is an offence against reason, truth, and right conscience" (No. 1849). If considered according to this definition of sin, the papacy is practically an institution of sin. Garry Wills, a Catholic historian, discusses the papal sin in his book *"Papal Sin"* (2000) and calls the institution of the papacy "structures of deceit". He wrote, "The truth, we are told, will make us free. It is time to free Catholics, lay as well as clerical, from the pressures of deceit, the quieter corruptions of intellectual betrayal" (from the Introduction). The writer feels that the history of the papacy is, in a sense, one long story of a gigantic fraud which unfolded over a period of some 16 centuries.

Regarding "the forgeries", the Catholic theologian Hans Kueng writes:

"All these forgeries are not curiosities of the time, as papal historians well-disposed toward the pope want to make out, but have had an abiding impact on the history of the church. The forgeries, most of which were subsequently legitimized by the pope, still appear in the Codex Iuris Canonici revised under the supervision of the curia and promulgated in 1983 by John Paul II."

I have quoted this earlier. The Codex Iuris Cananonici (Latin, the Code of Canon Law) is a vast complex legal system which has played a vital role in maintaining the pope's centralized control of the Roman Catholic Church throughout the world. Such a canon law did not exist in the apostolic church and in the churches of early centuries.

Regarding the Catholic doctrine of the Apostolic Succession, I point out that in the New Testament the apostle is not an office holder, but a first-hand witness to Christ, his words, deeds, death and resurrection. Being irreplaceable and unique, the apostolate cannot be transmitted to or succeeded to by subsequent generations. The New Testament compared the apostles to the foundation stones of a building (a metaphor of the church), Christ being the chief Cornerstone. Ephesians 2:20, cf. Revelation 21:14.

The laying of foundation stones is done at the beginning of the construction and is not repeated. In this world, things like a crown of a king, property and some kinds of legal power can be inherited from the present possessor by someone of the next generation, or transferred from one person to another. To give a useful analogy, it is like the impossibility of transferring the musical genius of Beethoven or the poetical genius of Goethe to someone else.

Similarly, even if the primacy of the apostle Peter were admitted, his primacy would be unique to him and not transmitted to the next generation. Accordingly the Catholic dogma of the pope's primacy as Peter's successor is biblically unfounded. The uniqueness of the apostolate was specifically mentioned by Christ himself. Our Lord said, "I tell you the truth, at the renewal of all things, when the Son of Man sits on his throne in heavenly glory, you who have followed me will also sit on twelve thrones, judging the twelve tribes of Israel" (Matthew 19:28).

We should not lose sight of or forget the uniqueness of the apostolate which is emphasized in the New Testament. We can legitimately use the term "apostolic succession" only in the sense of pure and true preservation of the apostolic testimony and teaching.

Our considerations so far lead us to conclude that the above-mentioned threefold claims of the Roman Church regarding the papal primacy are unsubstantiated deduction from Matthew 16:18-19. There is one more point which makes the claims of the Roman Church look even more untenable.

In the gospel of Matthew there is a saying of Jesus which creates additional difficulty for the controversial Roman interpretation of Matthew 16:18-19. It is recorded in Matthew 18:18. Whereas in the first passage (16:18-19) Jesus appears to confer authority to Peter alone, in the second passage (18:18) he confers authority on all apostles without differentiation. Jesus seems to be saying the same thing in John 20:22-23 as well. In addition, Ephesians 2:20 and Revelation 21:10, 14 also clearly indicate that all twelve apostles are the foundation of the Church. According to these passages, all apostles, not just Peter alone, are the foundation on which the Church is built and all of them received the keys of heaven to "bind and loose."

As mentioned already, the intense struggle within the Church which has lasted for many centuries was the struggle of the successive bishops of Rome (popes) to claim and establish the papal supremacy over all other bishops, and to concentrate the absolute power in their own hands. They succeeded in the West completely by the 13th century. Subsequently the pope's struggle continued to expand the papal dominion over the Church throughout the world, but it achieved only a partial success. Yet the existence of the papal rule of the Roman Church around the world indicates that it has had a remarkable success indeed.

But is this a true kind of success? The popes also attempted and struggled hard to gain and keep the political power as well, but to their disappointment, failed to keep it. Rome's insatiable lust for power and tenacious claim to the supremacy reveal a pagan spirit. It is the spirit of the ancient Romans that conquered the world around the Mediterranean and built the Roman Empire. Only in such a pagan spiritual climate could such a papal claim to the supremacy be made and gratification found in the wielding of power and domination.

In contrast to that climate, the spirit of Jesus is revealed in his saying I quote it again. Our Lord told his disciples:

> *You know that the rulers of the Gentiles lord it over them, and their high officials exercise authority over them. It shall not be so among you. Instead, whoever wants to become great among you must be your servant, and whoever wants to be first among you must be your slave – just as the Son of Man did not come to be served, but to serve, and to give his life as a ransom for many.*
>
> <Matthew 20:24-28>
> (See also Matthew 23:10-12.)

It is obvious that the Roman Church interpreted Matthew 16:18-19 and a few other favored biblical passages in terms of legal power and domination. This legal interpretation is incompatible with the spirit and teaching of Jesus.

We have seen that there are manifold difficulties with the monarchical papacy and the hierarchy of the Roman Church. We saw already that there is no historical evidence that the bishop of Rome exercised such a power in the earliest centuries. The monarchical papacy developed gradually in the course of history due to the historical and geographical situation and the will of the pope for power. We saw earlier that the popes used a series of audacious "forgeries" (forged historical documents) as a means to achieve their goal. If the primacy of the bishop of Rome was recognized since the earliest time as Rome asserts, we wonder why the use of multiple forgeries and the intense power struggles were needed. There has been no adequate explanation of this from Rome. Rome has only made claim after claim.

The pope and the hierarchical church (which is a clerical institution of different ranks from the pope downwards) claim to have the divinely invested absolute power, and enforce submission. The Roman Church claims that it is endowed with a threefold exclusive authority: first, the infallible teaching authority (the Church being the depository of saving truth); second, the authority to administer through sacraments the divine grace which is necessary for man's salvation; third, the authority to be the divinely authorized arbiter of man's fate after death, with the power to control through the mass and absolution man's period of stay in the pains of purgatory, and the power to enable him to go to heaven. The Roman Church claims to have the power to dispense saving merit from "the treasury of surplus merits" of the Virgin Mary, the saints and Christ which are at its disposal. Thus every Catholic has to depend on the Church for his or her knowledge of saving truths, for divine saving grace, and for the benefit of the treasury of merits. So the Roman Church is the arbiter of man's fate. What a difference between this aggrandized powerful Church and the church in the New Testament as the humble and lowly people of God and the modest "bride of Christ" who calls on the name of the Lord Jesus Christ!

This threefold claim of the Catholic Church should not be confused with the threefold claim of the pope, which we have discussed earlier. If a religious institution equipped with the powers just described is once established, it is in a position to dominate people with absolute power.

In the Roman Church the dogma of the papal primacy is not an isolated dogma, but is integrally linked to other major doctrines – the doctrines of the church, the apostolic succession, the sacred hierarchy, the magisterium, the infallibility of the church, the sacraments and the indulgence. The credibility of each of these doctrines and of the Roman Catholic Church is at stake with the truth or otherwise of the dogma of the papal primacy. It is a puzzling phenomenon that this pagan institution with the name of the papacy still thrives and rules in the name of Christ approximately one half of the total number of the Christians in the world. In this troubled world many hard-to-explain things take place. Observed phenomena like this and our knowledge of the history of religions and the churches necessitate the reassessment of the organized institutional religions and the churches.

XVII

THE CATHOLIC DOCTRINE OF THE SACRAMENT LACKS THE BIBLICAL BASIS

THE HISTORICAL FACTS AND EVENTS such as the Croatian Catholics' brutal atrocities committed to the non-Catholic Serb Christians and the despicable behaviours of the Catholic Church and Catholics with respect to the inhumane unjust institution of slavery and slave trade, serve as a disproof of the claimed efficacy of the sacrament of the Catholic Church in sanctifying its recipients (Catholics) and also throw discredit on the grandiose sacramental system of the Roman Catholic Church. I wish to present the biblical passages which, in my view, confirm our proposition.

I question the way the Roman Church legitimizes its ecclesiastical, sacramentalist religion by way of a particular interpretation of John 1:14 ("The Word became flesh.") and of Paul's concept of the church as the body of Christ, because the ecclesiastical, sacramentalist theme does not belong to the central theological thought of John and Paul.

Also the Roman interpretation of the Incarnation of the Word and of Paul's concept of the church is in my view biblically dubious. I ask the reader to note that I am not saying that the ecclesiastical, sacramentalist religion of the Roman Church is based on the Church's interpretation of John's and Paul's teachings in the New Testament. That is not the case. In the history of the Roman Catholic Church the ecclesiastical, sacramentalist system had developed first and only afterwards were its theological theories formulated to legitimize it. Obviously this procedure is an aberration, because the study of the Scripture and listening to what it says should come first, rather than "use" the Scripture afterwards to make up theological theories in order to legitimize what has been in existence for centuries. This is similar to the case of the monarchical papacy. The monarchical papacy had developed first; its theological theorizing came afterwards to legitimize it. This also is an aberration. We have discussed this question in chapters 1, 5 and 7.

Such being the case, the Roman Church's interpretation of the biblical passages which it asserts as referring to the church and the sacrament inevitably becomes manipulative because it reads its preconceived notions into the biblical passages. We call this a manipulative interpretation of the Scripture. If this is really what has happened, it means that a colossal evil has been committed by the Roman Catholic Church.

A fundamental question with regard to the sacrament is whether the sacrament is a sign and symbol of the invisible grace of God, or a channel (a means) of sanctifying the believers.

Of these three points, I think that the first and the second point have been made obvious to some degree through the narrative so far. In the following I am going to discuss the third point.

In comparison with other religions and other Christian churches, the Roman Catholic Church is clearly an ecclesiocentric and sacramentalist religion. The ritual sacramental system occupies the central and predominant place in the life of the Church and in the devotional life of faithful individual Catholics. There are seven sacraments in the Catholic Church: baptism, confirmation, eucharist, matrimony, penance, holy orders, and extreme unction.

The *Catechism of the Catholic Church* says, "The purpose of the sacraments is to sanctify men, to build up the body of Christ and, finally to give worship to God" (No. 1123). "Celebrated worthily in faith, the sacraments confer the grace that they signify. They are efficacious because in them Christ himself is at work" (No. 1127). By "efficacious" is meant that the sacraments work effectively, sanctifying the recipients and enabling them to love God and men and to be partakers in the holy divine nature, thus making them fit for blissful life in heaven. Even before going to heaven the sanctifying process has already started thanks to the objective *efficacy* of the sacraments of the Roman Church. It is also claimed, "Outside the Church there is no salvation" (Extra ecclesiam nulla salus). I make one more quotation from the *Catechism*. "The Church affirms that for believers the sacraments of the New Testament are necessary for salvation ... The fruit of the sacramental life is that the Spirit of adoption makes the faithful partakers in the divine nature ..." (No. 1129).

Through these quotations from the Catechism we see the important place the sacramental system holds in the Roman Church and in the lives of individual Catholics. We also see that the Catholic Church ascribes real effectiveness to the sacraments (especially to Baptism and the Eucharist, namely, the Mass) in sanctifying the recipients and making them Christ-like men and women. It is asserted that "the sacraments act *ex opera operato* ... It follows that the sacrament is not wrought by the righteousness of either the celebrant or the recipient, but by the power of God" (No. 1128).

Comment

In the nature of the case, it cannot be proved or known for certain whether or not the sacraments of the Catholic Church have real efficacy in making the recipients become morally better and Christ-like persons. We are keenly interested to see the evidence that the sacraments do indeed have such sanctifying effect. The assertions of the Catholic Church do not quite convince us of this efficacy. Not yet. Also we do not believe that the New Testament teaches plainly the sacramental efficacy in that sense. We would like to see the observable concrete fruits of love, changed life, sanctity and Christ-likeness. But we do not believe that we have seen more of such things in the predominantly Catholic communities and nations than in the non-Catholic regions. The Roman Church has canonized many men and women as saints, but we are not convinced that being canonized by the Catholic Church is the proof of their genuine sainthood.

We are inclined to think that the story of the Catholic Croatians' atrocities and savagery against the Orthodox Serb Christians and Jews amounts to a disproof of the efficacy of the Catholic sacraments and that it discredits the Catholic doctrine of the sacraments.

Here is another piece of what amounts to a disproof, in our view, of the efficacy of the sacraments of the Roman Church. It is the despicable behaviour of the Churches (both Roman and non-Roman) with respect to the cruel and unjust institution of slavery and the slave trade. It is a sobering historical fact that many millions of innocent Africans were kidnapped at gunpoint and sold as slaves. Cruelty, injustice and tragedy (from the Africans' point of view) involved in the practice of slave trade and slavery are beyond description.

The selling of Africans as salves against their will started in the 15th century with approval of the pope of Rome, Martin V and Nicholas V. A century later popes Paul III and Pius V forbade Catholic missionaries to have any part in the slave trade. Yet some Jesuit and Dominican priests continued the profitable trade. We have discussed this in chapter 3.

To make a long story short, neither the Catholic Church nor the Catholics, nor the non-Catholic churches, publicly condemned and openly opposed slavery and salve trade. In time there were a small number of individual Christians who realized the cruelty of slavery and the slave trade, and opposed them.

In the eighteenth century the movement against slavery was taken up seriously by the Quakers. The Quaker preacher John Woolman led a long campaign until his death in 1772. The Quakers' official title is "The Religious Society of Friends" and in some parts of the USA they are called "The Friends' Church". This religious sect originated in Britain and Ireland and spread to Europe and America. Lester Scherer, a historian of slavery, wrote a book on the history of slavery in America. I quote the first two passages from the book. "Only a few Christians, all of them Quakers, declared that slavery was incompatible with the Christian life for both salves and slave-owners." "By contrast, the most effective anti-slavery church was the Society of Friends ... Self-proclaimed and widely recognized as the nation's "conscience", the churches appeared to be saying that drinking whiskey or enjoying sex without marriage was more scandalous than holding people as slaves."

I draw attention to the fact that the Quakers have no ordained ministry, no set liturgy and creeds, and no sacraments as such. They do not believe in them. Therefore the Quakers do not have the benefit of sacraments. But they are devout Christians and have regular religious meetings. Although they are small in number, the Quakers have been widely known for their commitment to the promotion of peace and justice, and penal reform. In 1947 the Nobel Peace Prize was given jointly to the Friends Service Committee.

The shining example of love and Christian conscience of the Quakers as manifested in their movement against slavery (in contrast to the disappointing behaviour of the churches, Catholic and non-Catholic) lead us to a realistic appraisal of the institutional churches and their sacraments. We wonder, What is the use of the exalted sacraments of the Roman Church if "the sacramental grace" which is asserted to be efficacious *ex opera operato* do not produce the fruits of love in realistic terms among its recipients? We value the fruits of love and passion for social justice. We do not have much faith in abstract doctrinal theories of the institutional churches. We regard the contemptible behaviour of the institutional churches and their adherents with respect to slavery and the slave trade as a piece of disproof of the efficacy of their sacraments. It is extremely significant that the Quakers do not have the ordained ministry and the sacraments. How would the sacramentalists explain the love of fellow-man and the passion for justice of the Quakers, and the disappointing behaviour of the Roman Church and the Catholics?

Are not the passion for justice and acts of love what God consistently demanded through His prophets, namely, justice and mercy? Which side will be favoured by God in this respect, the Quakers or the institutional churches? God also said, "I desire mercy, not sacrifice" (Hosea 6:5). We have already seen this in the preceding chapters.

Jesus said, "Beware of the false prophets, who come to you in sheep's clothing, but inwardly are ravenous wolves. You will know them by their fruits" (Matthew 7:15-16). Also in his teaching about the Last Judgement, our Lord said, "I tell you the truth, whatever you did for one of the least of these brothers of mine, you did for me" (Matthew 25:40). But He (the Judge) will say to those on his left side, "Depart from me, you who are cursed, into the eternal fire prepared for the devil and his angels ... I tell you the truth, whatever you did not do for one of the least of these (brothers of mine) you did not do for me. Then they will go away to eternal punishment, but the righteous will go to eternal life" (Matthew 25:41, 45-46). The poor Africans who had been enslaved were among the least of the brothers of Jesus. We think that we have the authority of our Lord Jesus Christ that in the Last Judgement of God, both the righteous deeds and the sins of omission are the criteria of the Judgement.

In the New Testament we have a warning that the Judgement of God will begin with the church (I Peter 4:17). This is a warning to the authoritarian, self-aggrandizing church and its self-exalting hierarchy, and to other complacent churchmen.

In the foregoing chapters I have discussed in some detail and given a few reasons why I do not have much trust in some of the doctrines of the Roman Catholic Church. This is not unrelated to the issue we are considering in this chapter, but has some bearing on it, reinforcing my argument regarding the dubious efficacy of the sacraments of the Roman Church.

A shocking new report by a French news agency provides another piece of disproof. *Agence France-Presse* reported on March 23, 1977 that there were one million prostitutes in Italy and that in Rome alone there were 100,000 professional prostitutes. The Vatican and St. Peter's Basilica are located in Rome. Apparently the Holy See and a large number of holy places do not have spiritual and sanctifying effect as expected. The French news agency said that the numbers were given by an Italian women's organization for social morality. If this report is true, what does it seem to imply?

I give one more example of such disproof. The New York Times, on October 4, 1998, reported the result of a survey of the perceived degree of corruption of 85 countries conducted by an agency. I give a near duplication of the report written by the reporter, Barbara Crossette.

Transparency International, a small independent organization that has been tracking for four years how the public and international businesses view corruption worldwide, has published its largest survey to date, looking at 85 countries and ranking Denmark as the cleanest.

The 1998 Corruption Perception Index, like its predecessors, is a "survey of surveys," using a combination of studies of countries by how they are perceived.

The impressions this year are that of the top ten countries in the least corrupt category – Denmark, followed by Finland, Sweden, New Zealand, Iceland, Canada, Singapore, Netherlands, Norway and Switzerland – all but three are European. None of these ten least corrupt countries has traditionally been known as a Catholic country. All of them except Singapore and Switzerland have been known as Protestant countries. In Switzerland the Protestant and the Catholic populations are roughly the same in number.

At the other end of the scale, from the bottom up, are Cameroon, Paraguay, Honduras, Tanzania, Nigeria, Indonesia, Colombia, Venezuela, Ecuador, Russia, and Vietnam and Kenya in a tie.

Of these countries at the bottom Paraguay, Honduras, Colombia, Venezuela and Ecuador are in the predominantly Roman Catholic continent of Latin America.

The United States falls behind most European countries and Hong Kong, tying with Austria at 17th place. Transparency International is not alone in drawing attention to corruption through its branches in all parts of the world. In September, 1998 the United

Nations Development Program and the Organization for Economic Cooperation and Development joined hands to publish a study of anticorruption initiatives in 25 countries that serve as models in the battle against bribery, money laundering and other impediments to economic growth. But there is a new historical development today which makes things complicated, making our judgement difficult and even making our discussion so far look obsolete.

The New York Times published what it called an "Archive Article" on October 13, 2003 with the title, "Faith Fades Where It Once Burned Strong". It also gave an abstract of the 3,083 word article written by the reporter Frank Bruni. The abstract said in part, "The Changing Church Focuses on Christianity in Europe in the last quarter century. It finds withering of Christian faith in Europe and shift in its center of gravity to Southern Hemisphere; this is true in Roman Catholic Church as well as mainstream Protestant denominations …"

We would like to see the sanctified life of more individual Catholics and a noticeably higher moral standard of the predominantly Catholic communities and nations than elsewhere. It we see that, we will reconsider our present low evaluation of the sacramental system of the Roman Catholic Church.

XVIII

THE CATHOLIC CHURCH'S DOGMA OF TRADITION IS "A CONTEMPT OF THE WORD OF GOD"

THE IMMACULATE CONCEPTION AND THE Ascension of the Virgin Mary, the Transubstantiation of the elements of the Eucharist, Purgatory, the Primacy and the Infallibility of the Pope, and the dogma of Tradition – these are the dogmas which are unique to the Roman Catholic Church. These dogmas are not based on the plain teaching of the Holy Scripture.

At the fourth session (1546) of the Council of Trent (1545-63) which was convened by the pope Paul III in order to counter the Protestant Reformation and to deal with the issues deriving from it, the Council declared that the Council "receives and venerates with equal piety the books of the Old and the New Testament, and also the tradition concerning faith and morals as if dictated either orally by Christ or by the Holy Spirit and preserved by continual succession in the Catholic Church." Thus the unwritten "tradition" and the written books of the Holy Scripture were formally put on the same level of authority in respect to faith and morals. So the tradition was elevated to be an additional source of the divine revelation along with the Holy Scripture by the Roman Church. This indicates that the Catholic Church has realized that there are dogmas in the Church which are not taught in the Scripture. The Church of Rome felt the need of some means of legitimizing the unbiblical doctrines and ecclesiastical polity. The dogma of Tradition was devised to meet this need.

But that the Roman Church elevated "tradition" to be a new source of the divine revelation is a serious alteration of the traditional rule of the Church from the beginning. More seriously, this dogma of tradition contradicts the teaching of Christ who condemned the Pharisees for giving equal status to tradition alongside the Scripture. The situation is parallel. Christ condemned the Pharisees because they broke the command of God and nullified the word of God for the sake of their tradition (Matthew 15:6). Jesus said to the Pharisees, "Why do you break the command of God for the sake of your tradition?" (Matthew 15:3). The doctrines taught by tradition are "the commandments of men" (Matthew 15:9; Mark 7:6-7).

It is a surprise that the Roman Catholic Church ignored Christ's stern warning with respect to tradition. The Council of Trent put "tradition" on the same level with the Holy Scripture. But if it came to an issue between the Scripture and tradition, it was the Scripture that had to give way. Accordingly, in practice the Catholic Church places tradition even above the Scripture. If both are theoretically at the same level, the Scripture can no longer be the test for tradition.

In Colossians 2:8, the apostle Paul too warns against falling prey to what he called "philosophy of empty deceit" according to "the tradition of men". Likewise in Galatians 1:14, 16 Paul says that he abandoned his ancestral traditions when God reveled His Son in him. The apostle also says, "Do not go beyond what is written" (I Corinthians 4:6). "What is written" in this context probably refers to the apostolic testimony and teaching in writing. Peter placed Paul's writing alongside the Holy Scripture of the Old Testament (II Peter 3:15-16).

In the letter of Jude, the brother of James who probably was also a half brother of Jesus (Galatians 1:19), we read:

"Beloved, while I was making every effort to write you about our common salvation, I felt the necessity to write to you appealing that you contend earnestly for the faith which was once for all delivered to the saints."

<Verse 3>

Here Jude is urging the people of God to contend for and adhere to "the faith which was once for all delivered to the saints." Implied in this urging is that any addition to the faith which was one for all delivered to the saints or any change of the content of the faith is impermissible. "The faith which was once for all delivered to the saints" is based on the apostolic testimony, teaching and the Holy Scripture.

In the Church the apostolic testimony was a norm of doctrine. The apostolic testimony was not left to the recollections of the apostles alone. There was the guidance of the Holy Spirit; hence it was the testimony of the Holy Spirit as well. This theme is expounded in the great commissioning discourse (John 14-17) which Jesus gave at the Last Supper with his disciples. The apostles were to bear witness from their long acquaintance with Jesus, and the Holy Spirit also bears witness to him (John 15:26-27). Jesus promised them that the Holy Spirit would remind them of his words (John 16:13). Therefore the apostolic testimony and teaching are the norm of the doctrines of the Christian Church.

The apostolic doctrine of the Christian Church did not originate merely with the apostles' witness from their recollections but also with the guidance of the Holy Spirit. In the apostolic witnesses there were a common content and a principle which in hindsight we would call a theological principle. As it is so, even the chief apostle (Peter) could be withstood by a colleague when he betrayed the fundamental principle of the Gospel. (Galatians 2:11)

Above I said that the fact that the Roman Church elevated

"tradition" to the status of revealed truth along with the Holy Scripture is "a serious alteration of the traditional rule of the Church from the beginning". An elaboration of this statement is in order. The traditional rule of the Church from the beginning in this context concerns the doctrinal authority of the Church. To be more specific, it concerns whether the Church has authority to make a new doctrine (an article of faith) in addition to "the faith which was once for all delivered to the saints." The traditional understanding was that the Church has no such authority. I explain by giving examples. The apostolic age was followed by the age of the Church Fathers. It is necessary to examine what the Fathers taught with regard to this question.

St. Athanasius (296-373), the bishop of Alexandria, was a champion of the apostolic faith against Arianism and other heresies. Athanasius emphasized that "in the Holy Scriptures alone is the instruction of religion announced – to which let no man add, from which let no man detract—which are sufficient in themselves for the enunciation of the truth." To this statement the other Fathers would have given a cordial assent because the Fathers did not derive even one article of faith from the tradition outside the canon of the Holy Scripture. This has been historically attested. The Anglican bishop and theologian Charles Gore said, "I have never seen even one passage in any of the Fathers which contradicts this."

Another well-known Fathers, St. Basil (329-379) wrote, "it is a manifest falling from the faith, and a proof of arrogance, either to reject any of those things that Athanasius and St. Basil quoted above The teachings of the two Church Fathers were cited by Bishop Gore in his The Holy Spirit and the Church, 1924, p.173.) In our view this statement of Basil is applicable to the Roman Catholic Church that made a new dogma of Tradition in 1545 and has several more dogmas which have no biblical basis. In matters such as custom and discipline the Church could act freely as circumstance demands, but in the matter of the articles of faith the Church can do nothing except to preserve and teach "the faith which was once for all delivered to the saints."

The Council of Trent claimed that "the tradition concerning faith and morals … (has been) preserved by continual succession in the Catholic Church." But this is merely a claim. We recall that the Gnostics, too, a major heretical sect in the early Christian centuries which posed a serious threat to the Church, claimed to have a special gnosis (knowledge) which derived from the apostles by a "secret tradition". The Church strongly denounced it. There is akinness between the two claims. The Roman Church has not been able to produce the concrete content of this tradition which has been allegedly preserved in the Catholic Church from the beginning and which is not in the written books of the Holy Scripture. Furthermore, if there were such tradition preserved in the Church from the beginning, it would more likely be in the Eastern (Orthodox) Church rather than the Western (Roman) Church because the East, not the West, was the main theatre of the activities of the apostles. But the Orthodox Church of the East does not make such a claim as the one made by the Roman Church in the West. I repeat that the Catholic Church has failed to present the concrete of the tradition allegedly preserved in that Church.

In time the Roman Church's definition of "tradition" changed. To trace the change of the definition of tradition in the Roman Church is beyond the scope of this book. Instead I quote two theologians regarding this question. The Anglican theologian Charles Gore again writes, "'tradition' means what at any period the Roman Church has come to hold, whatever the records of the past may be" (ibid. p. 208-9). The Catholic theologian August Bernhard Hasler also discussed this question in relation to the dogma of Infallibility of the Pope in particular. He writes, "'Tradition' to them (the defenders of the dogma) means no more than the prevailing opinions of the Church's magisterium. Perhaps they advanced this version of church tradition because that was what the dominant curial party wanted it. The curial party demands that the Bible be expounded along the lines acceptable to the teaching authority of the Church, that is, of the pope. In its constitution on faith the First Vatican Council explicitly sanctioned this ecclesiastical monopoly on interpretation" (How The Pope Became Infallible, 1979, by August Bernhard Hasler, p. 177).

Thus the definition of "tradition" changed in the Roman Church according to the need of the Church, especially of the pope. This reveals what kind of authority the pope wields in the Roman Catholic Church. It approaches despotism. Indications of papal despotism are not scarce. An example is the pope's decree that scholars must stop the historical investigation about the past of the papacy and the Church. On September 1, 1910 the pope Pius X issued the motu proprio (pope's letter) "Sacrorum antistitium", imposing on scholars an oath disavowing Modernism. Scholars were also compelled to make an oath by December 31 of the year to discontinue their historical investigation because their investigation was a peril to the doctrines of the Church. Most scholars took the oath under pressure, but there were about two dozen who hesitated to do so. They were subjected to the inquisition in Rome and there ensued a widespread harassment of them.

The redefinition of "tradition" according to the needs of the pope and the prohibition of historical research are just two examples which indicate the papal despotism. Why was the order to discontinue historical investigation necessary? The pope perceived that the historical investigation by scholars posed a threat to the papacy. The Catholic Church could not stand a historical scrutiny of scholars. Does this imply that Pius XX was aware that there was something about which to be embarrassed in the past of the papacy? So the past needed to remain hidden for the sake of the safety of the papacy. The fact that many items in the Vatican archives were destroyed arouses a similar suspicion. If there was nothing to hide, why was such a measure needed?

Earlier I quoted the church historian Adolf Harnack's statement regarding papal tyranny and ecclesiastical despotism. I quote again, "(The papacy) developed itself into the *autocratic* power in the Church ... ... and framed its legislation by means of numerous decretals. The pope afterwards, till the time of Innocent III, defended and strengthened their position in the Church amid severe but victorious struggles. No doubt, they had to hear many an anxious word from their most faithful sons; but the rise of the papacy to despotic power in the Church, and thereby to dominion over the world, was promoted by piety (of the faithful sons) and by all the ideal forces of the period" (History of Dogma (1900) by Adolf Harnack, Volume VI&VII, pp. 17-18).

There is another important related issue. God gave the Ten Commandments through Moses. The Second Commandment says, "You shall not make a carved image for yourself nor likeness of anything in the havens above, or on earth below, or in the waters under the earth. You shall not bow down to them or worship them" (Exodus 20:4; Deuteronomy 5:8). Yet, in most Catholic churches there are a number of images (representing Jesus, Mary, angels and saints). In St. Peter's Basilica of Rome, for example, one can see many images (statues). Is it right to place those statues in the church or anywhere if people are not told to bow down and venerate them? The Second Commandment clearly says, "You shall not make a carved image ... ..." Also, is it absolutely certain that no one adores any of these images in his or her mind? It appears that many Catholics frequently bend their knees before the statue of Mary, for example, and pray to it. These statues could be a snare to idolatry for the "weak" members of the Church. "Laying a snare" for the people of God was strictly forbidden by God in a variety of circumstances, for example Exodus 23:32-33, 34:12-13; Deuteronomy 7:25-26, 12:30; Joshua 23:11-13; Judges 2:2-3, 8:27.

The Roman Catholic Church is showing a contempt for the Word of God in allowing multiple images to be made and placed in the church, in putting the Holy Scripture and the tradition on the same level of authority, and in having a number of unbiblical dogmas of the Church. As far as its observable behaviours are concerned, the Roman Church has not demonstrated its respect for the word of God. Therefore what the prophet Isaiah said with regard to the ancient Israelites is relevant to the Church of Rome, "They rejected the law of the Lord of hosts, and despised the word of the Holy One of Israel" (5:24).

It can be said that in the Roman Catholic Church the pope and the Church have been made idols in that the papal church has exercised an authority not less than divine and claimed an allegiance such as men owe to God alone. The excessive self-aggrandizement and self-importance of the self-appointed "Vicar of Christ" and the Church approach "the idolatrous self-worship" spoken of by Reinhold Niebuhr.

Aware of the charge of idolatry, the Catholic Church attempts to justify its practice about images by invoking the Incarnation of the Son of God. The Catechism of the Catholic Church says, "By becoming incarnate, the Son of God introduced a new economy of images" (No. 2131). This is another example of that "inference" from the Incarnation whereby the Church of Rome tries to justify its new dogmas and practices which the Church in the apostolic times had not heard about. There is nothing in the New Testament which indicates or implies such an idea. Does the Incarnation of the Son of God justify adoring even the statues of Mary, other saints, and angels?

In hindsight we see that God provided the Holy Scripture as a safeguard against the tyranny of authority (such as the pope and the authoritarian church) in order to preserve the purity of the true religion and morality. The attempt to alter the Gospel of Christ started already in the days of the apostles. The apostle Paul gave a stern warning against such an attempt. Cf. Galatians 1:6-9. Also he said elsewhere, "Do not go beyond what is written" (1 Corinthians 4:6).

There is an exact parallel, in our view, between the provisions of the written laws of God through Moses and the provisions of the apostolic testimony and teaching in writing. Both are God's provisions. Commanded by God, Moses wrote down the laws of God and said to the Israelites of his days:

> *"Take this Book of the Law and place it beside the ark of the covenant of the Lord your God. There it will remain as a witness against you. For I know how rebellious and stiff-necked you are. If you have been rebellious against the Lord while I am still alive and with you, how much more will you rebel after I die?"*

> <Deuteronomy 31:26-27>

Moses also said:

"Whatever I command you, you shall be careful to do; you shall not add to nor take away from it."
< Deuteronomy 12:32 cf. 4:2>

The situation in the days of the apostles and in the later days was similar. As we noted above, there were already attempts to change the Gospel of Christ while the apostles were still alive. The apostle John also wrote at the close of Revelation, warning neither to add nor to take away from the "the words of the prophecy of this book" (Revelation 22:18-19). The Gospel truth was already in danger of being altered and perverted. Therefore the written Scripture was an absolute necessity as a safeguard against human attempts to alter the true religion of God.

God provided this, namely, the Old and New Testament. With divine foresight and wisdom God commanded Moses and other prophets to write down for the posterity the word of God they received. For example, God said to the prophet Isaiah, "Go now, write it on a table for them, and inscribe it on a scroll, that for the days to come it may be an everlasting witness" (30:8). For another example:

The word came to Jeremiah from the Lord, saying, "Thus says the Lord, the God of Israel, Write all the words which I have spoken to you in a book."
<Jeremiah 30:1-2, cf. 36:1-4>

God who spoke to His people through the prophets and Christ have made His words thus spoken available to His people of later generations. So He has provided the Holy Scripture. If the revelation given is truly God's revelation, the Scripture as the record and testimony God gave to attest His revelation must be trustworthy. There is a remarkable passage in Isaiah which calls for our attention.

Seek and read from the book of the Lord:

Not one of these shall be missing;
None shall be without her mate.
For the mouth of the Lord has commanded,
And His Spirit has gathered them.

<34:16>

The Spirit of God has gathered the content of the Holy Scripture. If the mouth of the Lord has commanded and the Spirit of God has gathered the content of the Scripture, the status of the Holy Scripture is unique. Then what would the status of "tradition" be, which has allegedly been in the Catholic Church? How is the Catholic dogma of "tradition" to be assessed, according to which the tradition and the Holy Scripture are equal as the source of the Divine revelation? This Catholic dogma which was designed as an afterthought to legitimize those doctrines and practices in the Roman Church which are not found in the Scripture, is contempt of the Word of God.

In the Middle Ages the Catholic Church tried to keep the Holy Scripture away from the lay people. In a meeting in Toulouse (France) in 1229 the Roman Church formally forbade the lay people to possess or read the Scripture. For a layman to possess or read the Scripture was an offence punishable severely. During the five-century long Inquisition the offender was tried and put to death by burning. Until a few decades ago, the general tendency in the Roman Church was to discourage the reading of the Bible by laity. The picture today is not clear, varying to a degree from country to country.

In our view this is contrary to the will of Jesus our Lord. In the Synoptic gospels we count at least 14 passages in which our Lord approvingly refers to the reading of Scripture. We cite a few:

"Have you not read this Scripture?"

<Mark 12:10>

"Is this not the reason you are mistaken, that you do not understand the Scripture?"

<Mark 12:24>

"Have you not read in the book Moses how God spoken to him ...?"
<Mark 12:26>

"Have you not read that He Who created them from the beginning made them male and female ..."
<Matthew 19:4>

"What is written in the Law? How do you read it?"
<Luke 10:26>

Jesus sometimes called the Scripture "the law and the prophets" or "Moses and the prophets" (Luke 24:27, 16:29, 31).

How are we to interpret these sayings of Jesus? Our interpretation is that these sayings imply that:

1. Our Lord took it for granted that every person had a right to read the Scripture.
2. Our Lord assumed that his hearers had or should have had some knowledge about the content of the Scripture.
3. It is not right that people's access to the Scripture is barred by any authoritarian body.

We find in the Scripture that it is God Himself who has provided the Holy Scripture, and that God's purpose in providing the Scripture is that His People read or hear the words of God and obtain true knowledge about God and His ways. Cf. Deuteronomy 31:9-13. Those ancient Israelites at the time of Moses who were not able to read and for whom the words of God in writing was not available, were to hear others read the words of God for them.

How are we to view the decision of the Catholic Church that strictly forbade the people to read or possess the Holy Scripture? In our view such behavior of the church hierarchy is despotic, and amounts to disobedience to and an insult of God's command who gave these and other prescriptions about the Scripture. Is the pope really the Vicar of Christ and the Infallible teacher of the Christian Church as he claims? We must say a firm "No."

XIX

THE APOSTOLIC SUCCESSION AND THE THREEFOLD MINISTRY OF THE ROMAN CATHOLIC CHURCH

THE TERM "APOSTOLIC SUCCESSION" REFERS to the proposition that the ministry of the Christian Church is derived from the apostles by a continuous succession of bishops. The Roman Catholic Church holds the doctrine of apostolic succession and claims that this succession has been maintained by a continuous series of bishops from the beginning. The Orthodox Church and part of the Anglican Church also hold this doctrine. Bishops of these Churches are fond of calling themselves "successors of the apostles." Bishops of the Catholic Church are so-called "monarchical bishops". In the Catholic Church the doctrines of apostolic succession and of monarchical bishops are inseparably tied. The Catechism of the Catholic Church says, "Just as the office which the Lord confided to Peter alone, as first of the apostles, destined to be transmitted to his successors, is a permanent one, so also endures the office, which the apostles received, of shepherding the Church, a charge destined to be exercised without interruption by the sacred order of bishops" (No.862).

But these dual claims made by the Roman Catholic Church are not supported by the biblical evidence. Here we limit our attention to the claim that the bishops have by divine institution taken the place of the apostles. (The claim of the papal primacy will be dealt with separately in Appendix D.)

Most scholars who have studied this issue are of the opinion that the claim of the Roman Church cannot be substantiated by the Scripture. The term "apostolic succession" is not found in the New Testament and there is no clear indication of the idea in the New Testament. Acts 20:17, 28 and Titus 1:5-7 reveal that the office of elder (presbyter) and the office of bishop (episcopes, overseer) are interchangeable, which means that in the days of the apostles the elder and the bishop were identical. They were mature Christian men who were appointed to supervise the local church (I Peter 5:1-4). Then, gradually one elder, probably the teaching member of the group, assumed presidency to become the "bishop" with special powers and honour. This is a later development. During the lifetime of the apostles, this did not take place. In the New Testament, the bishop is not a different office from the elder. There are more passages which throw light on this question. Cf. Philippians 1:1; I Timothy 3:1-4, 8-13. Therefore we can say safely that in the New Testament the episcopate (the office of bishop) is not a distinct, higher officer above the presbyter (the elder).

There is a near consensus among non-Catholic theologians that the Catholic doctrines of the apostolic succession and the monarchical bishop have no biblical, nor church historical basis. Even some open-minded Catholic theologians admit this. For example Hans Kueng writes, "A careful investigation of the New Testament sources in the past hundred years has shown that this church constitution, centered on the bishops, is by no means directly willed by God or given by Christ, but is the result of a long and problematical historical development. It is human work and therefore in principle can by changed" (Hans Kueng: *The Catholic Church*, 2001, p.19).

Another Catholic theologian Piet Fransen expressed a similar view. He has made a historical study of the development of various ministries in the apostolic and post-apostolic Church. His is a rather comprehensive and basic study and therefore is worth quoting. "The Churches founded by Paul and others, like the Church of Rome, gradually came to have a governing body, called elders (presbyteroi) and later bishops (episkopoi), as in Acts ... These Churches developed more slowly towards the monarchical structure adopted in Asia Minor. This delay seems to be attested by Clement of Rome and in *Hermas*, and still later in the customs of the Churches of Alexandria and perhaps Lyons, where the installation and ordination of the bishop was the work of the elders. These customs may have lasted till the 3rd century. This evidence does not permit us to affirm that the hierarchy of orders, e.g. monarchical bishop, college of elders and deacons, was a divine institution in the strict sense, or even an institution of the apostolic Church, considered as a norm of later Churches."

Fransen's account is valuable because it is based on biblical and historical evidence. The fact that his presentation is contained in the Encyclopedia of Theology edited by Karl Rahner (1975) is significant since Rahner is a highly respected theologian in the Roman Church. (p. 1128)

If what I have presented above is true, then not only the doctrine of the apostolic succession of the Roman Church but also the doctrine of the threefold ministry of bishop, priest (elder) and deacon is to be questioned, and even the Roman Church's dogma of the papal primacy is not beyond dispute. The Catholic Church's claims about these hotly disputed issues are made in, for example, No. 880 and 881 of *the Catechism*. "When Christ instituted the Twelve, he constituted (them) in the form of a college or permanent assembly, at the head of which he placed Peter, chosen from among them. Just as by the Lord's institution, St. Peter and the rest of the apostles constitute a single apostolic college, so in the like fashion, the successors of the apostles, are related with and united to one another ... This pastoral office of Peter and other apostles belongs to the Church's very foundation and is continued by the bishops under the primacy of the Pope."

In our view, the evidence in the New Testament is not supportive of the Catholic claim. As we are not able to discuss all aspects of this controversial issue here, we will limit our consideration and focus on the main point. According to the New Testament, the apostolate is a unique office and as such cannot be shared with others or passed on to the later generations. Regarding the uniqueness of the apostles I quote an explanatory account in the Ryrie Study Bible (p.1460), "The word 'apostle' means 'one sent forth', and ambassador who bears a message and who represents the One who sent him. The qualification included:

1. Seeing the Lord and being an eye-witness to His resurrection (Acts 1:22; I Corinthians 9:1);
2. Being invested with miraculous sign-gifts (Acts 5:15-16, 14:3, 19:11-12; Romans 15:18; II Corinthians 12:12; Hebrews 2:3-4). Of these passages, I quote only one here: 'The things that mark an apostle – signs, wonders and miracles – were done among you with great perseverance' (II Corinthians 12:12);
3. Being chosen by the Lord or the Holy Spirit (Matthew 10:1-2; Acts 1:25-26)."

Healing and other miraculous gifts, such as prophecy and exorcism, are abundantly attested in the apostolic church, related, like the apostolic witness, to the special dispensation of the Holy Spirit. But they are missing in the post-apostolic church. Do the pope and the bishops of the Catholic Church perform miracles? Also the apostle's authority depended on the fact that he had been commissioned by Christ either in the days of his flesh (Matthew 10:5, 29:19) or after he had risen from the dead (Acts 1:24, 9:15).

The apostle Paul says, "The Church is built on the foundation of the apostles and prophets" (Ephesians 2:20). The apostle Paul is using a metaphor of building here and likens the Church to a house or a building. As everyone knows, foundation stones are laid on the ground at the beginning of the construction of a building or a house. Laying of a foundation is not repeated; therefore no more foundation stones are needed for the building. The foundation stones will sit and remain there and cannot be succeeded to or inherited by others in later generations. Ministers of the Church, no matter how distinguished they may be, cannot be foundation stones of the spiritual building called the Church. They are bricks, lumber or tiles of the building, so to speak. The foundation stones are to be clearly distinguished from the bricks, lumbers and tiles. According to Revelation, the last book of the New Testament, the names of the apostles are engraved on the twelve foundation stones of the Holy City, Jerusalem, coming down out of heaven from God (Revelation 21:14). Our Lord said that the apostles will sit on twelve thrones when He sits on His glorious throne at the Last Judgment (Matthew 19:28).

Thus the apostolate is a unique position and office. No minister of the Church can rightly claim to be a successor of the apostle. The Church of Rome has formulated its doctrines of the episcopacy and the papacy based on false claims including this one. The doctrine of apostolic succession is to be rejected as biblically unfounded.

Based on chapter 12 of I Corinthians, Romans 12:6-8 and Ephesians 4:11-12, theologians have presented what they perceived to be the apostle Paul's concept of the Church and the ministry of the Church. The Pauline churches were largely communities with free charismatic ministries. According to Paul "every" Christian was endowed with his appropriate gift of the Spirit for his own ministry (I Corinthians 12:7 and 11). So in the Pauline churches there were various forms of ministry: for preaching, teaching, giving help, administering pastoral care and so on. These were all necessary "for the equipment of the saints for the work of service (ministry)" (Ephesians 4:12).

But after the apostolic times, there gradually emerged a class of clergy who were increasingly separated from the people; the lay people came to be dominated by the clergy who monopolized ecclesiastical offices and tasks. This represents a deformation of the ministry in the New Testament sense of the word. The development of Eucharistic worship provides a good illustration of this deformation.

According to Paul's first epistle to the Corinthians, the Eucharist (the Lord's Supper) was initially part of corporate worship in which everyone had a role to play and each was as important as the other. But soon after the departure of the apostles the Eucharist became something celebrated by the priest (presbyter, episcopes) alone in the presence of the passive people who were looking on. Thus a radical change in the concept of the ministry and of the celebration of the eucharist took place. Gradually the Roman Church as a sacerdotal, ritualistic (sacramentalist) church dominated by the clergy emerged and was established.

According to the Catholic doctrine, the order of clergy is essential for the Church. But the New Testament conceives of the Church as the people of God; hence the clergy is not an essential part of it. This can be seen in, for example, Acts 14:23 and 20:28. As we have already discussed the latter passage, we limit our attention to Acts 14:23. Paul and Barnabas "appointed elders in every church" of South Galatia. Implied in the passage is that the churches were there before elders were appointed in them. Clergy are not essential to the Church in the sense that the Church cannot exist without them. Of course, some ministry is necessary in the sense that the Church cannot be fully effective for its tasks without it. In Rome, too, at the time when the apostle Paul wrote his epistle to the Christian community in Rome, there was apparently no order of clergy (bishop or elder) yet. We turn to consider the next related question, How and when did the so-called monarchical episcopacy as we see it in the Roman Church emerge? There is some mystery about the origin of the episcopacy. We saw earlier that in the days of the apostles the episcopos (the overseer, the bishop) of the church was not a distinct higher officer above the presbyter (elder). The two terms were interchangeable.

But early in the post apostolic period the threefold ministry of bishop – presbyter – deacon emerged. What is certain is that this threefold ministry appeared "after" the departure of the apostles. I quoted above the two Catholic theologians Hans Kueng and Piet Fransen who presented the view that the episcopacy in the sense of the monarchical bishop has no biblical basis and is not a divine institution. I quote Kueng again, "it cannot be verified that the bishops are successors of the apostle in the direct and exclusive sense. It is historically impossible to find in the initial phase of Christianity and unbroken chain of laying on of hands from the apostles to the present-day bishops. Historically, rather, it can be demonstrated that in a first postapostolic phase, local presbyter-bishops became established alongside prophets, teachers, and other ministers as the sole leaders of the Christian communities; thus a division between "clergy" and "laity" took place at an early stage. In a further phase the monarchical episcopate, of an individual bishop, increasingly displaced a plurality of presbyter-bishops in a city and later throughout the region of a church ... The Eucharist could no longer be celebrated without a bishop. The division between clergy and people was now a fact" (ibid. p. 21-22).

So for St. Ignatius (the bishop of Antioch in the early 2nd century), bishop, presbyter and deacon were already distinct. The threefold ministry also emerged in some churches of Asia Minor. By the middle of the 2nd century it appears that the monarchical episcopacy was adopted in major centres of Christianity in Asia Minor. Probably Ignatius was the first monarchical bishop in Syria and he is the earliest witness to the threefold ministry. The bishop became the supervising leader of a number of local churches in a region (later a diocese), not just of one local church. The leader of a local church was the elder (presbyter).

A crucial point to note is that Ignatius did not say that the episcopacy is a divine institution, and he does not mention the apostolic succession. Instead he emphasized the bishop's unifying authority in perilous times when the Church faced a crisis due to the heresies of Donatism, Gnosticism and Judaistic teaching which were rapidly spreading. He seemed to be saying that the monarchical episcopacy was the best way for the Church to weather the difficult times.

Through historical research it has been confirmed that the apostolic succession as a theory of ministry in the Church was absent in the 1st century and in much of the 2nd century. It arose during the last quarter of the 2nd century. All succession lists were complied late in the 2ne century. Clement of Rome (a contemporary of St. Ignatius of the East) appeals to a simple form of apostolic succession, but his letters betray no knowledge of the monarchical episcopacy and the threefold ministry of the church. In his famous letter to the Corinthians Clement makes it clear that for him, that is, in Rome and in Corinth, the titles "bishops" and "presbyters" refer to the same persons. Clemet's letter is regarded as extremely valuable in tracing the development of "early Catholicism" in the West. There was some difference in the development between the East and the West.

The apostolic succession in the sense meant by the Roman Church nowadays appears to be first found in the West in the 3rd century. We have a "testimony" of Jerome, a famous biblical scholar and translator, from the 4th century, "The presbyter is the same as the bishop, and before parties had arisen in religion, the churches were governed by the Senate of the presbyters." (Anderson Scott: Romanism and the Gospel, 1937, p. 149)

As I mentioned above, long before the time of Jerome the movement had begun which led to the setting of one bishop above his copresbyters. The movement started in the East and spread to the West.

The apostolic Succession as claimed by the Roman Church regulates not only the ecclesiastical government and the teaching authority of the Church, but also the liturgy namely, the sacramental system of the Church; and virtually the entire religion of the Catholic Church. Therefore if the doctrine of the Apostolic Succession turns out to be biblically and historically unfounded, it means that the grand edifice of the Roman Catholic Church is actually made of clay.

In any case, the New Testament is not concerned to indicate the method of transmission or succession of the ministry of the Church. Does this mean that things like the shape of the ministry and the constitution of the Church are secondary matters and they can be devised by the Church to meet its needs under varying circumstances? The main concern of the New Testament is to ensure that the apostolic faith, which is possible only through preserving and adhering to the apostolic testimony and teaching be deposited in its writing. The distinguished New Testament scholar F.F. Bruce rejects the Catholic doctrines of the apostolic succession and the apostolic church as biblically groundless and false, and says, "The true apostolic succession is the steadfast continuing in the apostles' teaching and fellowship. An apostolic church is one in which the apostolic teaching is maintained ... Provision is made in the New Testament for the maintenance of a true apostolic succession in this sense; see, for example, II Timothy 2:2, where Paul instructs Timothy to impart the teaching which he had received from Paul to faithful men, who shall be able to teach others also. So the continuity of apostolic teaching would be maintained from generation to generation, the canonical Scripture providing a permanent standard by which the apostolicity of this transmitted teaching would be tested. It was to safeguard the pure transmission of the apostolic teaching that emphasis was first laid on the importance of the continuous succession of bishops in a church, especially in a church of apostolic foundation" (F.F Bruce: Answers to Questions (1972), p. 154).

Our inevitable conclusion is that the apostolic succession of persons, the monarchical episcopacy, and the threefold ministry of the Catholic Church are man-made institutions.

We saw above how the division between "clergy" and "laity" (people) took place early in the postapostolic Church. After the ecclesiastical law of clerical celibacy was enforced early in the Middle Ages, the separation of the clergy from the people became more rigid and the priestly caste was firmly established. But according to the New Testament, the apostle Peter and other apostles took their wives along with them in their evangelistic journeys (I Corinthians 9:5).

As the ordained clergymen alone were authorized to celebrate the eucharist and other sacraments which were held to be the channels of the divine grace essential for salvation, the lay people were made powerless in the Church and dependent on and subordinate to the clergy. The Roman Church became a clerical church with a hierarchical, monarchical organization which culmincated in the autocratic papacy. The church as "the people of God", as taught in the New Testament, was ignored and pushed aside. Thus an imperious, authoritarian church emerged which may be regarded as the ecclesiastical version of the ancient Roman Empire as far as the structure of ecclesiastical government, jurisprudence and authoritarianism are concerned.

Printed in the United States
By Bookmasters